Lucas Mac-Uvre
New Haven, 2011

Political Theology

To Lucas,

will remain to be
convinced

[signature]

COLUMBIA STUDIES IN POLITICAL THOUGHT/POLITICAL HISTORY

Dick Howard, General Editor

Columbia Studies in Political Thought/Political History is a series dedicated to exploring the possibilities for democratic initiative and the revitalization of politics in the wake of the exhaustion of twentieth-century ideological "isms." By taking a historical approach to the politics of ideas about power, governance, and the just society, this series seeks to foster and illuminate new political spaces for human action and choice.

Pierre Rosanvallon, *Democracy Past and Future*, edited by Samuel Moyn (2006)

Claude Lefort, *Complications: Communism and the Dilemmas of Democracy*, translated by Julian Bourg (2007)

Benjamin R. Barber, *The Truth of Power: Intellectual Affairs in the Clinton White House* (2008)

Andrew Arato, *Constitution Making Under Occupation: The Politics of Imposed Revolution in Iraq* (2009)

Dick Howard, *The Primacy of the Political: A History of Political Thought from the Greeks to the French and American Revolution* (2009)

Robert Meister, *After Evil: Human Rights Discourse in the Twenty-first Century* (2011)

Political Theology

FOUR NEW CHAPTERS ON THE CONCEPT

OF SOVEREIGNTY

Paul W. Kahn

Columbia University Press   New York

COLUMBIA UNIVERSITY PRESS

Publishers Since 1893

New York   Chichester, West Sussex

Copyright © 2011 Columbia University Press

Library of Congress Cataloging-in-Publication Data

Kahn, Paul W., 1952–

Political theology : four new chapters on the concept of sovereignty / Paul W. Kahn.

p.   cm. — (Columbia studies in political thought/political history)

Includes bibliographical references and index.

ISBN 978-0-231-15340-9 (cloth : alk. paper) — ISBN 978-0-231-52700-2 (electronic)

1. Sovereignty. 2. Political theology. 3. Schmitt, Carl, 1888–1985. I. Title. II. Series.

JC327.K34   2011

320.1′5—dc222010025215

Columbia University Press books are printed on permanent and durable acid-free paper.

This book was printed on paper with recycled content.

Printed in the United States of America

c 10 9 8 7 6 5 4 3 2 1

References to Internet Web sites (URLs) were accurate at the time of writing.
Neither the author nor Columbia University Press is responsible for URLs
that may have expired or changed since the manuscript was prepared.

CONTENTS

FOREWORD

IT IS A PLEASURE TO ADD PAUL W. KAHN's book to the Political Thought/Political History series. This book broadens the reach of the series, whose premise, expressed in the editor's introduction to Claude Lefort's *Complications*, can be summed up in the phrase "no political thought without history, no historical thought without politics." Kahn's book suggests another set of complementary imperatives, "no politics without philosophy, no philosophy without politics." The Anglo-American discovery of the work of Carl Schmitt has unfortunately been more political than it has been philosophical. Kahn, a professor of law at Yale University, takes the opposite approach; concentrating on one relatively brief but central work by Carl Schmitt, *Political Theology*, he draws out philosophical implications of which Schmitt himself may not have been fully aware. What is more, he is able to do so because of his own intimate knowledge of American jurisprudence. By using simple examples from American legal experience, he shows that the radical reasoning that influenced Schmitt's own—bad!—political choices is founded on a philosophy of freedom that can be realized only when the freedom of philosophy is ensured. This, Kahn shows, is the central meaning of Schmitt's often-cited but equally often misunderstood definition of the sovereign as "he who decides on the exception."

Readers of this concise work will find not only that they come better to understand the thought of Carl Schmitt but also that they are helped to rethink the apparently self-evident values of liberal legal thought. They will have the pleasure of watching Paul Kahn interpret Carl Schmitt's famous argument that "all significant concepts of the modern theory of the state are secularized theological concepts" in a straightforward dialogue that Kahn skillfully sets up with Schmitt. By avoiding lengthy scholarly debate, political polemic, and exegetical erudition, Kahn has produced a critical work that joins politics and philosophy in a unique synthesis.

DICK HOWARD

ACKNOWLEDGMENTS

OVER THE COURSE OF THE LAST FEW YEARS, I have received advice and comments on this project from many, colleagues, friends, students, and even some strangers. More often than not, they disagreed with me. Still, they were generous in taking the time to deal seriously with the project. I greatly appreciated their encouragement, as well as their efforts to set me right. I tried to take in as much as I could, but there is much about which we will continue to disagree. I owe special thanks to my Yale Law School colleagues, Bruce Ackerman, Owen Fiss, and Robert Post. I also had the benefit of comments from two intellectual historians, Samuel Moyn and Jonathan Sheehan. As I get older, those who had been students become friends and colleagues. Several deserve special mention in connection with this manuscript: Ulrich Haltern, Benjamin Berger, and Mateo Taussig-Rubbo. The manuscript was the subject of a seminar at the Yale Law School, and I would like to thank the students of that class, who were unrestrained in letting me know what they thought. I especially want to thank Han Liu, Benjamin Johnson, Fernando Leon Munoz, Sophia Khan, and Kiel Brennan-Marquez for their help with the research. Thanks finally to Barbara Mianzo, upon whose administrative help I continue to rely.

Political Theology

INTRODUCTION

Why Political Theology Again

THE PROBLEM OF CARL SCHMITT

Carl Schmitt's *Political Theology: Four Chapters on the Concept of Sovereignty* is one of the most famous, as well as one of the most obscure, books in twentieth-century political theory. It is much cited by contemporary political and legal theorists, but those citations often seem to refer to just two canonical sentences: "Sovereign is he who decides on the exception" and "All significant concepts of the modern theory of the state are secularized theological concepts."[1] These are indeed critical claims, but standing alone they are as puzzling as they are shocking.

The claim of a theological origin for political concepts stands against the widely accepted belief that the turn away from religion by figures such as Locke, Hume, and Smith—not to speak of Machiavelli and Hobbes—laid the groundwork for the modern theory of the state.[2] The social contract, not the divine covenant, is at the center of modern political theory. The localization of sovereignty in a single subject who decides is similarly inconsistent with modern beliefs about the rule of law, separation of powers, and judicial review. Today, we are more likely to ask "what exception?" rather than who decides on it. How, after all, can we reconcile Schmitt's definition of sovereignty with that classic line of American jurisprudence, "extraordinary conditions neither create nor enlarge constitutional power"?[3] In a system of popular sovereignty, we do not know a "he" who can claim to be the sovereign; in our system of constitutional law, we do not know a state of exception.

Puzzling as these two famous sentences appear on first impression, most American readers have an intuition that Schmitt is pointing to at least some aspects of our political situation that are difficult to understand within the terms of contemporary political theory. We know, for example, that the American president is trailed by a military officer carrying a box with the nuclear attack codes. The President maintains a world-destroying power. Is this an example of the sovereign power to decide on the exception? Surely, such a decision would itself be exceptional not just in a political sense, but in a legal one as well. There would be no judicial review of the decision, no opportunity to challenge it by those affected, no due process, and no norm of law that the president could claim to be executing. Imagining such a moment of decision, we might find ourselves using religious concepts: Armageddon, for example. More generally, we are familiar with the idea that Americans practice a "civil religion."[4] Consider the Pledge of Allegiance, the iconography of the flag, or the memorialization of citizen sacrifice. These are only the most obvious elements of this practice.[5] How important are these aspects of our political life? And, what exactly is the relationship of faith to reason in our political practices? These too are political-theological questions.

Schmitt was, of course, not thinking of the practice of an American civil religion. Can his suggestions about political theology, nevertheless, help us to understand the way in which the modern nation-state—particularly our nation-state—has occupied the place of the sacred for its citizens? Does the idea of the constitution, for example, carry forward the religious concept of the covenant? Is revolution a secularized form of revelation? Are these examples of "secularized theological concepts"? Just to the degree that these questions remain plausible, we need a political theology to explore the sources and nature of our political life.

Schmitt links exception to sovereignty in his first sentence. Not just this text, but political theology as a form of inquiry begins where law ends. If today we are generally inclined to believe that we live in a world of law that is, or should be, without exception, is it the case that we live in a world without sovereignty? Much of the contemporary political theory of globalization claims exactly that: sovereignty, on this view, is an anachronistic concept that has become dysfunctional at best, and misleading at worst, in our world of human rights and global markets.[6] Neither the discourse of human rights nor that of economic markets has any room for the exceptional, sovereign decision.[7] For both, political order means law without exception. But is this like saying that under modern conceptions of science there is no longer a cognizable place for religion? In both cases, our theory of the universal claim of law—natural or political—may not match our experience of faith or our actual, institutional practices.

Even those who object to contemporary claims for a global order of law are more likely than not to share with liberal political theorists a skepticism toward claims for a theological approach to political analysis—unless of course, they are fundamentalists attacking the secular character of modern politics both locally and globally. The "antiglobalization" or "global justice" movements, for example, show little interest in the theological. The leftist critique of liberalism may rest on a deep philosophical difference concerning the nature of justice and the forms of oppression, but that debate avoids any claims for or about the sacred.[8] That political concepts have their origin in theological concepts is, to most contemporary theorists, about as interesting and important as learning that English words have their origin in old Norse. Consequently, a contemporary political theology must be more than a genealogical inquiry if it is to be more than a passing curiosity. It becomes interesting just to the degree that these concepts continue to support an actual theological dimension in our political practices. Political theology as a form of inquiry is compelling only to the degree that it helps us recognize that our political practices remain embedded in forms of belief and practice that touch upon the sacred.

Since 1922, when Schmitt wrote *Political Theology*, there has been a change in the background beliefs against which we understand the possibility of political theory. Theology is no longer an important element of philosophical inquiry in general and, at least in the United States, no longer a major aspect of the institutional life of the university. If political theology is about empowering theologians politically or theoretically, it has no future in the West. The very possibility of a political theology has been displaced from the academy by the rise of positive political science. Indeed, arguably this shift from theology to science, in the study of both nature and social practices, is what makes us modern. For us, the most pressing questions are likely to concern the relationship between liberal political practices and market structures. We think of ourselves as living in an increasingly multicultural world in which any effort to link politics to religion is likely to prove counterproductive, if not actually dangerous.[9] Religion belongs to civil society, where it is simultaneously protected and excluded from politics. In our discourse about politics, we speak a language of institutional structure and procedure, on the one hand, and of rights and welfare, on the other.

While questions of the relationship of law to religious practices and beliefs remain matters of controversy, academics have, for the most part, lost touch with the subject matter of Schmitt's book: political theology. If political theology means anything at all to us, it is associated with religious fundamentalists who oppose liberalism at home and are the enemies of the modern secular state abroad. Domestically, we are likely to associate political theology with those who insist that America return to its origins as a "Christian nation." *Our* political practices, on this view, should be measured by *their* religious beliefs. Externally, we are likely to associate political theology with Muslim theocracies: the Saudis have a political theology; Osama bin Laden attacks us in the name of a political theology.

When we try to put the two well-known Schmittian sentences back in their larger textual context, we are frustrated by the obscurity of the book. Our failure of understanding can be attributed, in part, to the form in which Schmitt presented his ideas. To the contemporary reader—especially the American reader—the book appears as a virtually impenetrable consideration of lost German theoreticians.[10] Their work, in turn, was responding to a political crisis of which we are only dimly aware. With a few exceptions—notably Max Weber and Hans Kelsen—there is little point in elaborating the views of those long-gone European theorists who occupied Schmitt's attention. Often, Schmitt is situating himself in the contemporary debate. These, however, are matters for the intellectual historian, not for the political philosopher.[11]

Adding to the obscurity of his text and the association of the entire endeavor with the domestic and foreign opponents of the modern, liberal state, we come to Schmitt with a skepticism and even animosity because of his personal politics. Schmitt associated actively with the National Socialists. How long he did so remains a subject of some dispute: he never formally left the party, nor did he disavow his earlier, active support. Schmitt scholars have argued endlessly about the depth and character of this association.[12] However one explains the connection, it is impossible to deny that he believed there to be a relationship between his theoretical work and his politics. We cannot but see a reflection of Schmitt's definition of the sovereign as "he who decides on the exception" in Schmitt's support for Hitler, who emerged so forcefully a decade after he wrote this sentence. Schmitt's understanding of his own work put him on the wrong side of history.[13] He personally illustrates the danger of his ideas; his own biography supports the association of political theology with fascism.

Of course, we should not overestimate the role of Schmitt in German politics, nor the influence of political theory on politics in general. Theory is rarely an effective form of political praxis; it does not translate easily into either effective rhetoric or a specific plan for action. One of the subjects of *Political Theology* is a consideration of just why this is so: between norm and application there must be a decision. Philosophers have no particular skills when it comes to decision; they are not trained to have good judgment. Philosophers have rarely been effective in politics: a fact already evident to Plato after his Syracuse experiment. Nevertheless, we are right to worry that the road from Weimar to National Socialism, at least in the domain of political theory, moved through Schmitt's political theology.

If an engagement with Schmitt is to be useful in the domain of theory today, we must put aside both the local context of his work—the Weimar crisis—and his personal political beliefs and practices. Lasting theoretical contributions will have their origins in local circumstances, but they do not depend upon those circumstances. Indeed, it misses the philosophical point and disrespects the political thinker if we emphasize context over content. Of course Schmitt wrote against a background of pressing, local concerns. So do we, but then so did Plato, Aristotle, and every other philosopher. Their achievement was to gain a freedom of thought within those circumstances. This is the attitude with which we must approach Schmitt's work. It is the same attitude with which we should approach any other creative work, whether of art, literature, or science. This is not an excuse for Schmitt's politics, which were inexcusable. Rather, the point is that no excuse is needed to engage the work. Taking up that work, we need not give any special weight to what Schmitt may personally have believed about his text.[14]

This work will inevitably be seen as part of the post–Cold War resurgence of interest in Schmitt. That turn toward Schmitt was puzzling. Just as a global regime of law—a regime that seriously threatened the traditional idea of sovereignty—was growing, so was interest in Schmitt, who was the century's leading theorist of sovereignty. For those who harbored some skepticism about the claims of a new world order, Schmitt became a useful resource. Skepticism toward a developing orthodoxy with respect to a global order of law was linked to a renewed interest in the place of violence in political culture.[15] Schmitt put the state's power of life and death at the center of his inquiry into the political. Along with Schmitt, Walter Benjamin became popular, and he too was often reduced to a few canonical sentences, including most famously, "There is no document of civilization which is not at the same time a document of barbarism."[16] Post-1989, Schmitt became a reference point for those who sought to develop a broadly antiliberal theory, free of the decades-old dispute between the communitarians and the liberals. Schmitt symbolized this new freedom from old categories, for while he was personally associated with the far right, those most interested in his theory traced the development of their own political views to the left.[17]

The fact that much of the enthusiasm for Schmitt followed the collapse of the Soviet Union should give us pause, for Schmitt may be our best guide to understanding the Cold War as an era in which political conflict threatened to break out into world-destroying violence. At stake was always more than the political theory of either the liberal or the Marxist variety could explain: mutual assured destruction could not be understood from the perspective of either a doctrine of rights or a clash over ownership of the means of production. To understand the political imagination of complete annihilation, we need a political theology. Had liberal theory, like socialist theory, served as an exercise in political apologetics? Did it require the end of the Cold War to free a space for a new form of critique of liberal theory in the West?

In truth, there was never much distance between liberal political theory, typified by John Rawls's *Theory of Justice*, and the American constitutional order.[18] America was a good enough political order when compared with its Cold War adversaries. Yet Rawls and his followers never took seriously the violence of the state. Mutual assured destruction never appears within liberal political theory. It is as if the violence of the United States is simply an accidental characteristic of an essentially liberal political order: a posture forced upon the liberal state by threats from abroad. The defense policies of the United States are always seen as somehow exceptional—more transitional arrangements than expressions of national identity. We constantly expect the defense budget to go down, not up; we are slightly embarrassed by the maintenance of a standing army. Whatever happened to the state militias which were to be called out in the rare case—the exception—of national emergency?[19]

If we are to understand state violence as no less an expression of political identity than law, then we must take a perspective upon ourselves other than that offered by liberal political theory. We must take up the perspective of political theology, for political violence has been and remains a form of sacrifice. This is not hidden but celebrated in our ordinary political rhetoric: to serve and die for the nation is commonly referred to as "the ultimate sacrifice." We can find no more obvious nor more important an instance of Schmitt's "secularized theological concepts." Moreover, the moment at which such sacrifice is performed is always that of the exception. Law can impose risks, but it cannot demand a sacrifice. Not even in the military is there a legal regime of the "suicide mission."[20] One way to express this is to say that sacrifice is always a free act. Liberal theory puts contract at the origins of the political community; political theology puts sacrifice at the point of origin. Both contract and sacrifice are ideas of freedom. The former gives us our idea of the rule of law, the latter our idea of popular sovereignty. On this difference turns not only the distinction of political theory from political theology, but also our understanding of ourselves and of our relationship to the political community.

The project I propose here is to reflect on our political beliefs, institutional structures, and patterns of behavior by engaging with Schmitt's *Political Theology*. The text was subtitled *Four Chapters on the Concept of Sovereignty*. Sovereignty remains critical to understanding the American political experience. It is, however, a concept that has dropped from sight in most contemporary political and legal theory. Schmitt's text can help us to recover that concept, but only if we keep in mind that the conversation with him is about us; it is not about him. My aim here is not to elaborate the meaning of *Political Theology* as he understood it. Rather, it is to engage his work as a point from which to illuminate our own political experience. Schmitt, the person, does not appear in my text at all. All references to him should be understood in the very narrow sense of the author of the text, and that is all.[21]

AMERICAN EXCEPTIONALISM AND POLITICAL THEOLOGY

To take up the perspective of political theology requires us not just to reconsider the character our political theory, but to consider how well contemporary theory maps our political imagination. A political theology—one that breaks free of religious fundamentalism—must straddle both philosophy and anthropology. It raises fundamental questions about the nature of contemporary experience and of the place of the political in that experience. It brings to that inquiry a set of concepts—faith, sacrifice, the sacred—that are ordinarily excluded from political theory.

These are not small issues. Before we turn to *Political Theology,* we must have reason to think that the work promises something more than a few quotable sentences that can be deployed to express contemporary frustrations with liberal theory and recent American political developments. In response, we might begin by noting that *Political Theology* speaks directly to the relationship between constitutional law and political sovereignty. For Americans, this is the problem of the relationship between the rule of law and popular sovereignty, that is, between law and self-government. Indeed, I can summarize the inquiry of this book in a single question: what do we learn if we engage Schmitt's argument from a perspective that substitutes the popular sovereign for his idea of the sovereign?

This relationship of law to popular sovereignty is the central problem of American constitutional theory, where it goes by the name of "the counter-majoritarian difficulty."[22] When the Supreme Court declares a law unconstitutional, what exactly is the source of legitimacy for that judgment? The ruling is not a judgment as to the justice of the legislation. A theory of justice will not get us very far in understanding this aspect of American political practice.[23] If we say the Constitution itself is the source of the Court's legitimacy, then how is it that a two-hundred-year-old text can deny a contemporary popular majority the right to rule itself? When the Court declares a law unconstitutional, it is invoking some sort of exception: its decision marks the endpoint of the ordinary course of legislative majorities responding to shifting political interests. Does our Court live within the matrix of the Schmittian exception?

That our Court occupies a role that has a theological dimension is an old point. At the center of our civil religion is the "priesthood" of the Court, guarding that most sacred of texts: the Constitution.[24] While the Court likes to appeal to the rule of law to legitimate its exceptional role, political theology suggests that we look in a different direction: to the Court's capacity to speak in the voice of the popular sovereign.

Not coincidentally, our belief that the Constitution is the product of popular sovereignty supports what is commonly called "American exceptionalism." American exceptionalism appears in our nation's reluctance to join international human rights conventions, to agree to submit itself to the jurisdiction of transnational courts, and to recognize claims of universal jurisdiction by foreign courts.[25] This resistance is puzzling for two reasons. First, it is often the case that these conventions and institutions are, in substantial part, products of American foreign policy efforts.[26] Second, we resist even though we do not disagree with the substantive content of most of contemporary international human rights law.[27] Nevertheless, we are reluctant to displace national law by international law. No doubt, there are sometimes narrow, self-interested reasons for avoiding international law, but resistance to the displacement of our own constitutional order is broad and deep. Americans have a problem imagining international law: if law is an expression of popular sovereignty, how can a system of norms that has no source in that sovereign constitute law?[28]

The concept of popular sovereignty links the Constitution—and thus the rule of law—to the Revolution; it links law to exception. The Constitution continues to express the revolutionary self-formation of the popular sovereign. The counter-majoritarian difficulty is resolved by an appeal to the presence of the popular sovereign. The judicial decision, accordingly, becomes the space for the exceptional reappearance of the sovereign. From this perspective, American exceptionalism may be best understood as a variation of the Schmittian exception. This is surely not what he had in mind, but we are playing the notes of political theology—including the idea of the exception—in a new key, that of popular sovereignty.

Political theology may not only help us to understand ourselves but also to understand how and why our political imagination makes our relationship to the rest of the world so exceptional. Americans resist international law not just because they do not see it as grounded in a legitimate act of popular self-determination, but also because it is law beyond sovereignty in the sense that it is law without exception. Many intuitively believe this is not a political arrangement within which America can survive as a nation. In our contemporary political debate, this is just the argument we have been having over the international law prohibition on torture under any and all circumstances. The American resistance to a rule without exception is expressed in the regular invocation of the ticking time bomb hypothetical. Implicit in the hypothetical is the idea that the bomb might be nuclear. Without an exception to the torture prohibition, we face the possibility of a nuclear detonation, that is, we imagine the death of the state. The issue here is not whether this belief is true, but how it figures in the construction of a broader political imagination.[29] That imagination is the object of political theological inquiry.

Americans continue to imagine a world in which there are potential enemies and thus one in which politics can turn to life-threatening violence. Ironically, the world's most powerful nation lives with a belief in

the insecurity of its own existence. This is ironic, but hardly odd. Political beliefs are not a matter of reason alone, and there can be no assertion of power that does not harbor a reflexive fear of failure. Schmitt believed that a world in which potential enemies are feared is not one that can be fully ordered by law. Thus, the European project of creating a transnational order of law without exception required that no national community view any other within the European Union as a potential enemy. Out of this comes the idea of European citizenship, as well as the limits on the potential extension of that idea.[30]

The identification of the enemy is not grounded in a difference in policy but rather in the perception of an existential threat.[31] In the face of such an imagined threat, one decides to act. One does not adjudicate national survival.[32] The exceptional turn to violence against the enemy will always be understood as the defense of sovereign existence. This includes, but is not exhausted by, the defense of the order of law that the sovereign put in place: to defend the state is not just to defend the border, but to defend a way of life. For Americans, the rule of law is not that which eliminates the need for the violent defense of the nation, but that for the sake of which violence is deployed. Paradigmatic of this synthesis for Americans was the Civil War, in which defense of sovereignty was inseparable from defense of the Constitution. The current war on terror shows us the continued vitality of these themes of law, exception, sovereignty, and the imagined existential crisis of the state.

Schmitt writes that the exception is more interesting than the norm because "it confirms not only the rule but also its existence" (15). An abstract rule is not defended; it has no existence. There is a sense in which the entire American political experience is lived within the exception—or at least within the shadow of the exception. The order of law begins in the exception of the Revolution and continues always under the possible need to turn to violence to defend the revolutionary accomplishment of a constitution. The translation of this imaginative construction into material reality today is found in the world-destroying power of the American nuclear arsenal. How is it that a political order that understands itself as characterized by the rule of law can hold forth the possibility of such destruction? A political theory that will not take the step to political theology is simply not equipped to answer this question.

Any theory of law that ignores the exception will fail to grasp the reality of American power and the nature of the American political imaginary. There is a direct line from the revolutionary consciousness of 1776 to the weapons of mass destruction today. That line passes through the popular sovereign and the Constitution, to arrive at our current debates over law and exception. The ticking time bomb example, as an argument for torture, is simply another imaginative construction of the Schmittian exception. When we imagine the time bomb as a nuclear weapon, we have replicated under current circumstances exactly the character of American exceptionalism throughout the Cold War.

The concept of the popular sovereign as an intergenerational, collective subject capable of action that is simultaneously creative and destructive is not accessible to someone who views the political culture from outside the terms of its own self-imagination. The sovereign is no more imaginable from without than is a god to those outside of the faith. A foreign faith's belief in the miraculous appearance of the divine is always reduced to a false or mistaken belief by those who are not prepared to see the sacred in those circumstances. We don't imagine that there were Aztec gods that have now withdrawn or that gods once lived on Mount Olympus. If the popular sovereign is a political theological concept, then it will no more appear to the contemporary political scientist than those earlier gods appear to the social scientist. In place of the popular sovereign, the political scientist today speaks of popular majorities and of the forces that effect electoral politics—all measurable entities.[33] There is no need for a separate concept of popular sovereignty, which will only obscure what needs analysis: voting trends, coalition building, and the competition for power among institutions and factions. The political scientist explores how judges participate in the formation of public policy: judges appear as only another locus of political power to be analyzed in the same way as other political institutions.[34]

From the perspective of the political scientist, the American practice of judicial review will not appear exceptional: judicial institutions in many countries review legislation for its constitutionality. European constitutional courts, for example, have no trouble declaring legislation unconstitutional. They do so, however, in the name of individual rights, not in the name of the popular sovereign. The American Supreme Court founds its claim for legitimacy on its capacity to speak in the voice of a transhistorical popular sovereign. The method of legal reasoning for European courts, on the other hand, is "proportionality" review, which is just another name for balancing the various interests—including rights—that are at stake in a situation. This is an all-things-considered judgment of the best way of moving forward given the conflicting claims and interests—exactly what a legislature should consider.[35] Because they operate on the same conceptual horizon as the legislature, judicial review has effectively been incorporated into the law-making process of European states: the best analysis of the law-making situation speaks of "governing with judges."[36]

One does not "govern with judges" in the United States: the imaginative horizon of constitutional decision making by the Court is entirely different from that of the legislature. Here, the Court speaks in the name of the popular sovereign. It is not a participant in ordinary politics but a presence outside of politics. Such a court relies on charisma—mystery and awe—as much as on argument. When seen as only another instance of ordinary politics, the Court's legitimacy is undermined. The best contemporary example of this may be the fear expressed by the dissenting justices as to how the Court's decision in *Bush v. Gore* would be perceived.[37]

The American legislature governs under the provenance of the Court, not with the Court.[38] Judicial review works as a reappearance of the political rupture: we are to hear once again the voice of the popular sovereign.[39] For this reason, the Court resists descriptions of its deliberative process as proportionality review—even though that is often what it appears to be doing.[40] Instead, it imagines itself to speak the constitutional truth. Only by taking seriously this idea of a national "truth" can we begin to make sense of the abiding appeal of originalism as an interpretative strategy.[41]

The divide here is not a matter of competence or knowledge. American and European justices are, for the most part, doing the same thing.

More than anything else, the different approaches reflect a difference between the secular and the sacred. No theory that avoids the theological can be adequate to the American practice of judicial review, which has its roots in the sacred character of the popular sovereign. Postwar American constitutional theory often tried to describe the difference between Court and legislature as one between decisions based on principles or enduring values, on the one hand, and those based on interests or short-term preferences, on the other. This was never convincing outside of the academy, for the Court hardly has a monopoly on the consideration of principles. Our deepest divisions—for example, over abortion, religion, or federalism—are all differences over principles. An academy that is no longer open to consideration of the theological will always confuse the sacred with the "principled"—perhaps because what is sacred to the academic is principle.

While the sovereign rupture has been successfully institutionalized in the practice of judicial review, this is not the only site at which the popular sovereign appears in tension with our ordinary legal practices. As others have pointed out, this tension was arguably behind the extraordinary claims that President Bush made to conduct the war on terror beyond the reach of the courts and the ordinary norms of law. The most controversial of the Justice Department memos placed presidential war powers beyond the control of law.[43]

In the United States, we generally find a deep skepticism of executive claims to act in the name of the people outside of law.[44] There are routine citations made to Lincoln's suspension of habeas corpus and to Roosevelt's extraordinary wartime efforts, but such instances are few. The revolutionary heritage has its roots in executive abuse; the Constitution was, in large part, an attempt to limit executive power. When we step back just slightly, however, we do see effective presidential power to decide upon the use of force—an area in which the courts have been most reluctant to intervene.[45] No president has accepted the constitutionality of the War Powers Resolution.[46] When we try to bring the reality of a president's world-destroying power under a theory of the constitutional allocation of power, we are falling exactly within a puzzle that Schmitt raises: Is the exception a concept within or without the order of law? Can a norm define the exception, or is it the other way around? How exactly is a decision that places itself outside of law nevertheless bound to law? The idea of the exception captures this conundrum, for we can only understand an exception by reference to the norm. If, however, we make the exception an instance of the norm, we lose the concept completely.

We are likely to have conflicting views, depending on the context, of whether the president or the Supreme Court has the power to decide on the exception. For that matter, the legislature also makes such a claim, for it has the formal, constitutional authority to declare war. Historically it has contested the president's claim to speak for the people. All three branches claim some sort of ultimate power to act in the name of "we the people."[47] Interestingly, while the Constitution specifies a single exceptional power, the suspension of habeas corpus, it neglects to specify who is to decide on that exception. We face the puzzling situation of action in the name of the Constitution, but outside of the ordinary structures of law, which always allocate jurisdiction when specifying power.[48] We can work Schmitt's equation backward to understand why, if the sovereign is he who decides, a system in which no political actor can make an uncontested claim to be sovereign is one that cannot localize the power to decide. The competition for the sovereign voice in American political life can take just this form of a competition to decide upon the exception. Is this not just what we have been seeing in the complex competition between president, courts, congress, and voters in determining the appropriate response to the threat of terrorism?

The defining conceptual struggle of our political age is whether the response to terrorism should be thought of as a matter of law enforcement ("a police action") or as a matter of war (an assertion of "sovereign power").[49] Are we within law or are we within the exception? That we can ask the question at all suggests that Americans have not accepted for themselves the postwar vision of Western politics as a matter of law alone. Our political culture is one in which both law and sacrifice figure, and in which the believer finds the truth of the self in and through participation in the popular sovereign. It is a faith that can support sacrificial violence as easily as it can support adjudication under law. Indeed, in the concept of the popular sovereign, we find the imaginative link between law and violence: at stake in both is the creation and maintenance of "we the people." America, we might say, finds itself equally when it looks to the court and the bomb.

Unsurprisingly, Americans and Europeans have given fundamentally different answers to this question of law or war. The juridification of politics is the leading idea of the Western European political order today. To the question of whether there can be sovereign action beyond the rule of law, European institutions have answered with a resounding no. All political violence is limited to law enforcement: no exceptions. Correspondingly, there has been a seamless movement from the order of constitutional law, with its protection of fundamental rights and limited delegations of power, to international law, with its prohibition on the use of force and its articulation of a doctrine of human rights.

There is no political theology appropriate for the institutions of the European Union: it is politics as a fully secularized practice of reason. Reason denaturalizes borders, just as it displaces the existential question from political life. The European Union is to pursue politics without sovereignty: law without exception.[50] The United States, however, never underwent any sort of postwar reconfiguration of either our political institutions or our political imaginations. We remained an "exceptional" nation because we never gave up our belief in our own sovereignty. Not surprisingly, the American triumph in the Cold War has been read—at home and abroad—through both the lens of law and that of violence, sometimes described as "soft" and "hard" power.[51]

Americans live comfortably with their long history of citizen sacrifice in national wars. American history begins with the Revolution and continues today in the war on terror. Popular history is shaped by a narrative of the successful use of violent force against enemies, within and without the nation. Much of this past remains vivid in our political imaginations, endlessly reinforced by both popular media and scholarly work. Americans take their families to Valley Forge and Gettysburg, and even to Omaha Beach. They do not think of past political violence through the prism of the concentration camp or the destruction of urban centers. They visit Mount Vernon and the Lincoln Memorial, not palaces like Versailles or camps like Auschwitz. They may visit the reconstructed slave operations at Monticello, but they do so believing in a myth of progress.

If sovereignty remains a concept necessary to constitutional law and to our practice of American exceptionalism, then we are not yet released from the burdens of faith. America, of course, remains a land of religious faith, while Western Europe has become a largely secular society. Faith in one form or another is a deep part of our political culture and of our political psychology. While law might be a product of reason and thus move easily from a national to a transnational discourse—the discourse of reason always claims universality for itself—self-government is a matter of will, which is always particular. To bring reason and will together remains the task of the constitutional theorist.[52] This task will require bringing jurisprudence in touch with theology. The product of that intersection is political theology.

Political theology then, may help us to understand the character of American exceptionalism in the full sense of the word: our exceptional political history of sustaining a two-hundred-year-old constitutional text, our practice of judicial review, our easy recourse to violence, and our willingness to sacrifice. We need to understand the set of beliefs that sustain and support American exceptionalism as a practice of ultimate meaning for generations of Americans. In our imaginations, political life remains a matter of life and death—that is exactly the meaning found in 9/11. We will never find an adequate explanation of the politics of sacrifice in liberal theory or positive political science.

POLITICAL THEOLOGY MISUNDERSTOOD

If we overcome an initial inclination to dismiss Schmitt's work as both dangerous and obscure, we should still be struck by the startling and indeed counterintuitive nature of the project of political theology. At the center of this project is the claim that the break between the secular and the theological is not what we might have thought. Mark Lilla has recently described this break as "the great separation" and put it at the origin not just of modern thought about the state but at the origin of the modern state itself.[53] To argue that our political practices rest on a civil religion is to claim that no such break ever occurred. There is continuity, not discontinuity, between the theological and the political. We should be very clear. The claim here is not that such a break should not have occurred and that politics must be put back on a religious foundation. That would be a normative intervention in politics. My enterprise is descriptive: to explore the political imagination we have, whether or not we should have it.

Obviously, something happened at the origins of the modern state. Some sort of change occurred when political leadership freed itself of the claims of the church. Whatever Schmitt meant by political theology, it cannot mean today that secular government is secretly doing the work of the church, or that it should. Nevertheless, for Schmitt, we only begin to understand the modern state when we place it in the theological tradition. For Lilla, on the other hand, understanding begins when we place the state against that tradition. Schmitt and Lilla are located in the same scholarly tradition. Yet, they understand the modern nation-state in diametrically opposed terms. To confront Schmitt is, accordingly, to confront the most fundamental issue in theorizing the character and meaning of the modern state.

Lilla describes "political theology" as the approach of those who believe that their religious faith must shape the political order. The serious claim of political theology today, however, is not that the secular should yield to the church—whatever church that might be—but rather that the state is not the secular arrangement that it purports to be.[54] A political life is not a life stripped of faith and the experience of the sacred, regardless of what we may believe about the legal separation of church and state. This is a far more radical claim than Lilla seems to imagine: not that the break should be repaired, but that the break never occurred. Political theology does not just challenge a particular configuration of legal institutions, as if the question were one of scaling down the wall of separation between church and state. It challenges the basic assumptions of our understanding of the meaning of modernity, the nature of individual identity, and the character of the relationship of the individual to the state.

The point of a contemporary political theology must be just the opposite of those premodern political theologies of which Lilla writes: not the subordination of the political to religious doctrine and church authority, but recognition that the state creates and maintains its own sacred space and history. Modern political theory began by imagining the state as the expression of a social contract that was the product of reasonable agreement among a group of individuals trying to escape danger and privation. On this approach, law is the answer to the coordination problems that arise in a state of nature. Political theology represents a challenge to this whole line of theory. Politics does not put the security of law in place of the violence of the state of nature; rather, it brings sacrifice in place of murder. Sovereignty is not the product of reason. It has nothing to do with agreement. Imagining the social contract is a theoretical enterprise that can only take place after the recognition of sovereignty. Sovereignty enables the social contract; the social contract does not create the sovereign. In Schmitt's terms, "the rule proves nothing; the exception proves everything" (15). Faith precedes doctrine. Put in more familiar, contemporary language, the argument over the just content of law occurs only within the ongoing enterprise of national existence.[55] We need, in short, to theorize both law and sovereignty.

If we mean by the great separation that the state must rest on its own bottom, that no religious authority has a privileged place in setting the political agenda, then political theology too is part of the modernist project. Its point, however, is that this separation is misunderstood if it is read as the disenchantment of the political world. Political theology is a project set against Max Weber's description of the bureaucratic, spiritless character of the modern welfare state. In such a state, the identity of the subject makes no difference: all subjects can be processed as holders of claims to which the bureaucratic administrators of the welfare state respond. This is not the world that Schmitt perceives when he gazes upon political experience. Of course, he sees evidence of bureaucratization, but this hardly fills the imagination of the political or constitutes the limits of political experience.

Schmitt's concept of the political begins with the distinction of friends from enemies. This is a world in which subjecthood—who you are—makes all the difference. While Schmitt's politics were completely objectionable, surely he was right to see that the immediate future of Europe was going to develop along the lines of this concept of the political and not that of administrative and bureaucratic rationality—more precisely, administration would be made to serve the ends of the political. A politics of friends and enemies is not a rational politics, for reason alone cannot establish this distinction.

Just as Freud argued that the modern idea of the individual as a self-determining, rational agent mistakes a normative theory for the reality of lived experience, Schmitt argued that the modern, liberal understanding of the state mistakes a normative theory for the phenomenon of political experience. We continue to make the same mistake, confusing a normative theory of liberalism with the lived experience of citizenship.[56] And, just as Marxists were surprised and disappointed when the laboring classes of Europe aligned with their individual nations rather than an international proletariat in the First World War, lately, political theorists have been surprised by the enduring power of national political identity in the face of rising claims for a new cosmopolitanism.

We Americans are still deeply wrapped up in this debate over the foundations of the political community: reason or identity? When, for example, we argue about whether to extend the privileges of the welfare state to immigrants—legal or illegal—the question is whether we should think of the individual from the perspective of universal need or from the perspective of membership in a historical community. Are individuals seen, in the first instance, as bearers of rights or as possible friends and enemies? The discourse of rights quickly moves to the level of the universal: human rights. That of friends and enemies insists that in politics there is no such universal perspective. Political theology cannot ignore claims of justice—there must still be a content to one's laws—but it explores the fundamental categories of the imaginative construction of self and other that are at stake in our political life.

There is no theoretical resolution of this conflict of perspectives because both appeal to first principles. We can argue that all subjects should be treated the same under law because all are entitled to equal respect and all have the same basic needs. But equally we can argue that membership in a community, whether familial or political, is not to be subordinated to an abstract idea of the individual subject. This conflict of first principles—justice or love—is the basis of the interminable argument between liberals and communitarians; it is now reappearing in the debate between liberals and multiculturalists.[57] There is no single answer to the question of how political groups conceive of themselves and their members. The right question is not theoretical at all. Rather, it is a question of how we place ourselves in relationship to these competing principles. We should begin with a kind of phenomenology of the political, which is just what political theology must be today.

Freeing the state from the church did not banish the sacred from the political. It might have, but it did not. The French revolutionaries attacked the church, but they found it necessary to invent their own rituals of the sacred. As with all revolutions of the modern period, the quality of the sacred was claimed for both the sovereign people and for reason. The French tried to establish a ritual practice that sacralized reason, but they did so in the name of the sovereign people.[58] The American Revolution practiced the same double forms of the sacred, worshiping "self-evident truths" set forth in the name of "We the People." The framers separated church and state but spoke the language of the sacred when pledging their lives to each other in their revolutionary mission. It is a safe generalization to say that all revolutionaries struggle with the relationship of justice, imagined as the universal norms of reason, to sovereignty, imagined as an experience of a particular community. This is why revolutionaries dream of "world revolution"—their vision of justice under law knows no limits—yet inevitably find themselves practicing an intense nationalism that identifies friends and enemies. This intersection of the universal and the particular has the familiar character of religious practice in the West, from the Jews as the chosen people, to Christ as the realization of universal justice in his singular act of sacrifice.

For both the French and the American revolutionaries—and all of their successors right through the recent Solidarity movement in Poland—the most serious threat to politics as a field of ultimate meaning came not from the church but from commerce. The competition with organized religion was a competition over the locus of the sacred; that with commerce was over the existence of the sacred. It is another safe generalization to say that all revolutionaries—from Thomas Jefferson to Lech Walesa—feared that they had lost their revolutions to commerce. Political revolutions are never powered by material need alone. Material need characterizes the state of nature; revolutions begin with a willingness to sacrifice.[59]

Revolutions begin with an experience of the sacred in and through the political, for no revolution begins until there is a willingness to sacrifice for some meaning greater than the finite self. But it does not demean revolutionary action to recognize that revolutionaries dream of well-being even as they give themselves freely to a politics of sacrifice. How could it be otherwise? That Christ offered bread to the poor did not make their beliefs less than spiritual. We want justice even as we sacrifice. Nevertheless, the revolutionary generation tends to judge its children too harshly. Neither in France nor in the United States did commercial success extinguish the imagination of the popular sovereign as a sacred presence that could demand a life. The postrevolutionary history of both nations remained one that moved easily between commerce and sacrifice, between the pursuit of individual well-being and violent destruction of that same individual. The bourgeois family had no problem sacrificing its sons in the great wars of the nation-state.

We often align law, welfare, and commerce, thinking that the point of law is to create a stable context for commerce that will satisfy the material needs of individuals. On this view, the creation and protection of property is at the center of law. Political action is seen as a supplement to action in the market; it is driven by the same interests and interest groups that operate in the market. Accordingly, political reasoning, like market reasoning, should demonstrate means-ends rationality.[60] At exceptional moments—most particularly revolution and war—this linkage of law to commerce gives away to an alternative idea in which political identity is linked to sacrifice. Politics at such moments becomes an end in itself and political reasoning is shaped by rhetoric, not logic. Politics becomes a matter of life and death, not of more and less. Money is no longer a placeholder for political power, which is generated, in Arendt's words, by great words and deeds.[61]

Political theology understands politics as an organization of everyday life founded on an imagination of the sacred. Both politics and religion share a rhythm of movement between the ordinary and the extraordinary—between norm and exception. Approaching politics from the perspective of the exceptional demand for killing and being killed, which has characterized the most intense moments of Western political experience, we can see that organized religion is just one form in which the experience of the sacred is named and embodied. The political formation of the experience of the sacred is the subject of political theology.

POLITICAL THEOLOGY AND LIBERALISM

To think that organized religions make a complete claim to the sacred—that is, claims title to all that is sacred—is to confuse legal categories with political phenomenology. It is an accident of history that the struggle of the state to free itself of the church was framed not as a conflict of faiths but as a conflict over the place of faith in the organization of political power. In part, this was a consequence of organized religion's tendency to side with conservative political forces. In part, it was because these political revolutions began two hundred years after the Reformation, which did indeed use the language of the sacred against the established Church. When modern revolutionaries took up the task of translating the felt meaning of political revolution into a constitutional order of law, they thought of themselves as men of the Enlightenment using the language of reason to push religion out of the public sphere. This hardly means that they neither experienced nor relied upon the sacred. In Arendt's classic analysis, they began by demanding legal rights but ended with an experience of the absolute character of public action.[62] Rights as a means to private ends became a lesser theme to the experience of a kind of transcendent meaning in and through political engagement. In a crisis, it remains true today that the secular state does not hesitate to speak of sacrifice, patriotism, nationalism, and homeland in the language of the sacred.[63] The state's territory becomes consecrated ground, its history a sacred duty to maintain, its flag something to die for. None of this has much to do with the secular; these are matters of faith, not reason.

The great separation of church and state was intended to place religion squarely within the private domain, outside of the public order of the state. Some supported this position on the grounds that it was good for faith, others on the grounds that it was good for the state, and some on both grounds. Some of our most troubling issues today arise from the crossing of this line of separation, for example, debates over the legal status of abortion or of gay marriage. These debates show us the porousness of the line, for the values we bring to public debate will inevitably reflect our basic beliefs about what it is we owe each other. Those beliefs come from all of our experience, including the ethical practices of our religious faiths.[64] Such tensions are something we all understand. Coming from a religious tradition of monotheism, however, it is much harder to understand a multiplicity of forms of the sacred. Indeed, to speak the language of the sacred about the state suggests not just a violation of the public/private divide, but to many it also suggests a practice of idolatry. Both the religious person and the secularist may agree that they want no gods in the public space: the former because there is only one god, the latter because there are no gods.

Political theology recognizes a multiplicity of forms of the sacred. If sovereignty is grounded in sacrifice, then public life is as much about the realization of a transcendent truth of the self as it is about the maintenance of a just legal order. Political theology, unsurprisingly, has no place in the liberal conception of the state, which begins with Lilla's great separation not as a historical fact but as a philosophical premise. This difference at the level of theory, however, does not necessarily produce any tension between political theology and the political practices of liberalism. If the political order maintains both an idea of the sacred and an idea of justice, of sovereignty and law, then the point of political theology is not to undermine a particular concept of justice but to expand the horizon within which we understand the operation of the political imagination. Liberal politics may strive to achieve a defensible idea of justice, even as liberal theory fails as an explanation of the source and character of political experience.[65]

The interesting way in which Schmitt was against liberalism had nothing to do with his personal political beliefs and practices, which were indeed antiliberal. Rather, his theory of the political denies the fundamental premises of liberal political theory. This is an argument over the nature of political experience, not over what we should or should not do within the polity. Although Schmitt may not have thought so, one can be liberal in one's personal political values and practices and still think that we need a theological account of political experience. This is no more difficult than practicing a politics of liberalism while recognizing the importance of revolution to the normative—and historical—foundation of the state. There is nothing liberal about revolution. The relationships at stake here are the political form of that which appears to the individual as the relationship of love to justice. The objects of our love do not earn our affection because they are just, but that does not make us indifferent to justice. We love our children and, therefore, we want them to be just. But we do not abandon our love if they act unjustly.

If we view politics through the lens of contemporary, liberal theory, we will misapprehend the nature of political experience and the meanings that citizens realize in and through their political identities. Elements of political experience grounded in faith and sacrifice will be ignored. We will always be surprised by the violence of which the state—even the liberal state—is capable. Liberalism as a theory of the political fails when political practice turns to killing and being killed, whether that violence is turned inward in the form of revolution or outward in the form of war. We will dismiss the high political rhetoric of sacrifice as dangerous, because it is unreasonable. But only according to liberal theory must the state be a "reasonable" enterprise. Political theology reminds us that apart from reason there remains faith—dangerous as that might be.

Political theology, as I pursue it here, is a project of descriptive political analysis. We are well past the era in which theology could draw upon reason to support the sacred. Indeed, that separation of reason from revelation may be a more important "great separation" than that of which Lilla writes. We will not be convinced by any logical arguments for the existence of God, whether the god of politics or that of religion. Theological inquiry today can only be a practice of phenomenology: to identify and describe the presence of the sacred, wherever it appears.

Political theology gains its critical edge when we juxtapose the products of that phenomenological inquiry to the constructions of liberal political theory. At stake is our understanding of the social imaginary by which we frame our world. There is nothing wrong with setting oneself against the values that are revealed in this account. We are not bound to our political experience as we are bound to the experience of the senses. Understanding the power of the nation does not make me a willing recruit. But unless one begins with an understanding of the character of the social imaginary, one's oppositional political practices are likely simply to miss their targets. Just as no one will be convinced by argument to believe in God, no faith was ever defeated by argument alone. The ground of faith is in the experience of the sacred, and this works quite independently of reason.

Political theology today is best thought of as an effort to describe the social imaginary of the political. It proceeds at the intersection of constitutional law, cultural anthropology, theology, and philosophy. The inquiry is not to take us back to premodern forms of religious influence on political order, but to the discovery of the persistence of forms of the sacred in a world that no longer relies upon God. Political theology argues that secularization, as the displacement of the sacred from the world of experience, never won, even though the church may have lost. The politics of the modern nation-state indeed rejected the church but simultaneously offered a new site of sacred experience.

By describing his work as theological, Schmitt suggests that the stakes involved are existential and phenomenological. Meaning, not efficiency—experience, not justice—is the issue. While he would no doubt vigorously object to the comparison, he is in some respects not so distant from that other existential explorer of the soul, Sigmund Freud. Both saw a culture desperately looking for possible sources of meaning in the face of a modern crisis of faith. Both doubted the capacity of reason to exhaust the sources of meaning that structure a human life. Schmitt, the constitutional lawyer, differed not so much in his concerns, as in the direction of his inquiry. For him, it was not the individual soul but the soul of the polity—of man in his political, rather than his psychological, aspect—that was the object of inquiry.

Schmitt's work invites us to develop a political theology for our time. We must pierce the state's self-presentation as an efficient means of justly advancing individual welfare and look to the experience of the political. Metaphorically, when we put the modern state on the couch, we find a social organism that is simultaneously deeply in fear of its own death (the existential crisis) and in deep denial of the fact that it is willing to do anything at all to put off that death (liberal theory). Looking into the soul of the modern welfare state, we can still see the *mysterium tremendum* of the sacred, with its tremendous power for both destruction and construction.

This work must be responsive to the particular conditions of an American superpower that simultaneously asks its young people to take up the political burden of sacrifice in the war on terror and seeks to affirm its belief in the rule of law. Many of our deepest conflicts—practically and conceptually—emerge out of this double commitment to a practice of political sacrifice and a practice of law. A sense that something has gone awry was expressed in the repeated critique that the Bush Administration did not ask the nation as a whole to take up the burden of sacrifice. We simultaneously condemned the war in Iraq as mistaken but felt that we should all be sacrificing more for the larger war on terrorism. Dissatisfied as we may be with that war, the problem is not that the nation will no longer respond to a call for sacrifice.

While liberal theory has given us tools to understand the rule of law, it has pushed out of sight the meaning of political sacrifice. To understand the latter, we must turn to something like Schmitt's ideas of exception and decision. If we imagine the decision as the result of a logical deduction, we will never leave law and liberal theory. The decision that is the act of giving up the self is never the result of logic. It is an existential choice to be—or literally not to be. We can study liberal political theory a very long time and never find this existential moment of self-sacrifice. We can turn from theory to law and still not see the plainest facts of our political life. If politics remains even in part a practice of sacrifice, then we must follow Schmitt into the domain of the theological.

THE PLAN

I propose an interpretive engagement with *Political Theology*. I will not offer a traditional interpretation of the text, trying to make clear

Schmitt's references to the obscure debates he pursued with his contemporaries. Rather, I will take up the central ideas of the text by thinking through the basic point of each chapter. Thus, the chapters that follow bear the same titles as Schmitt's chapters. My aim is to show how these ideas can still help us to understand the contemporary experience of the political. The point is not to become a Schmittian, whatever that might mean. It is, instead, to engage with Schmitt's text in order to offer an alternative approach to our own political experience. *I want to think with him, rather than think about him.* In the course of my analysis, I will consider the nature of philosophy as a free discourse. My "conversation" with Schmitt is intended to be a model of this understanding of philosophy. This conversation will move a considerable distance from Schmitt's own thought, but that is exactly what we should expect of a philosophical inquiry.

My aim is not to cast doubt on the liberal political practices of contemporary society. Properly approached, a phenomenological inquiry has no normative implications whatsoever for particular political controversies. Its ambition is to expose the common background of the political imaginary, which is shared by both sides of a controversy. Nor will the inquiry tell us what attitude to take toward the beliefs and practices described. We understand this when we consider a phenomenology of religious experience. To describe the phenomenon, even to stand deeply within it in order to grasp the manner in which it shapes the imagination is not to make any judgment whatsoever as to whether it is good or bad. We are free to take up a moral stance toward our own experience of meaning and condemn it as wrong. Of course, we need not do so.

Offering an alternative theory does, however, have normative implications for work in political philosophy. A bad theory should be replaced by a better one. Schmitt argues, and I agree, that much of liberal political theory misunderstands the character of political experience. It has an inauthentic understanding of the political. It is in flight from recognizing the centrality of sacrifice—of killing and being killed—to the construction of the political imaginary. To put, at the origin of political experience, the pledge to sacrifice instead of consent to the social contract has broad implications for political philosophy. Most importantly, it points us in new directions for understanding the character of freedom and the nature of the rule of law. Ultimately, it will ask us to reconsider the relationship between thought and action—not, however, in support of a plan of political reform, but as a matter of philosophical first principles.

The chapters that follow identify aspects of the modern Western political imagination that are still very much with us. These imaginative structures, to the degree Schmitt grasped them, were no more bound to his own understanding of how they applied to the political disputes of Weimar Germany than Plato's conceptualization of politics was bound to classical Athens or Rousseau's to revolutionary France. All of our theoretical ideas come from somewhere. Schmitt was, as we remain, a product of two millennia of Western experience of political life as not just a source of order but also of meaning. Western intellectuals have been trying for a very long time to understand both dimensions of the state: order and meaning. Liberal theory took a particular turn when it subordinated meaning to order—or as liberals like to put it, the good to the right. Schmitt's work often focused on the mismatch between that theoretical turn and the lived experience of what he called "the political." So do I.

My approach, then, is to engage Schmitt's text in an effort to uncover the phenomenon of the political. This work is neither an exegesis of his text, nor an intellectual history. Much of his short text is little more than a series of cryptic suggestions. My plan is to pursue some of these suggestions in an inquiry that is responsive to contemporary conditions. The product must stand on its own. I assume no familiarity with Schmitt's text and none with his historical situation. Thinking with him, I acknowledge an intellectual debt, but that is entirely different from claiming to be either an expositor or a disciple.

The task is to use the conceptual structures and imaginative relationships that we discover to interpret the political world in which we find ourselves. The relevant politics for us is contemporary. We have no reason to think that seeking some illumination from an engagement with Schmitt's text will lead us to replicate the political decisions that he made. All the evidence points in just the opposite way. We have even less reason to think that Schmitt would himself have approved of this use of his text, but neither should we care what Schmitt would have thought.

I

DEFINITION OF SOVEREIGNTY

THE OPENING WORDS OF CHAPTER ONE are some of the most famous in the history of political theory: "Sovereign is he who decides on the exception." This sentence sets up the structure of the entire inquiry and is thus the point of entry into a political-theological approach. That approach is a kind of mirror image of the political theory of liberalism: not law, but exception; not judge, but sovereign; not reason, but decision. The inversion is so extreme that we might think of political theology as the dialectical negation of liberal political theory.[1]

Reading the sentence nearly one hundred years after Schmitt wrote it, we still have to wonder about the success of the modernist project of subordinating all politics to law. We, who just barely survived the last century, may be similarly situated to Schmitt's generation, which had just barely survived the First World War. Reading Schmitt, one feels that he comes to the political with an awareness of its potential for violence, a sense that law is straining to contain that violence, but also a recognition that something terribly important is at stake in this violence: "The exception . . . can at best be characterized as a case of extreme peril, a danger to the existence of the state, or the like" (6). This is not the violence of the state of nature, but the violence of state creation and destruction. Surely, the contemporary problem of terrorism looks a good deal like a political situation in which law may fail, violence threatens, and meanings of great significance are at issue.

Three critical terms appear in this opening sentence: sovereign, decision, and exception. Each can be defined only in terms of the others; together, they point to a single political phenomenon. That phenomenon can best be approached by setting the opening sentence in contrast to the parallel proposition of three concepts: "the judge is he who applies the norm." These two propositions describe competing political imaginaries, that is, ways of understanding the character, source, and meaning of political experience. The second proposition captures the imagination of ordinary life in the modern, liberal state: order is the product of general norms expressed in and through law. These norms bind government actors and protect individuals from each other. Every individual can appeal to a judge to protect his or her legal rights. This model of legality, when linked to the democratic production of norms, is the source of legitimacy in the normal situation. The sovereign is displaced from view, lingering at best as a mere abstraction—popular sovereignty—but not capable of any concrete intervention.

Schmitt's opening proposition describes an entirely different imaginary, one in which norm and judge have been pushed from view. There is nothing abstract about the Schmittian sovereign: he decides in an act of will. The decision for the exception is distinctly not the application of a norm, which means that it will violate rights and interests recognized in the normal situation. Most dramatically, in the exception the sovereign will take life and property, while under ordinary circumstances legal norms protect life and property. Is this not exactly what happens in a war?

This opening sentence, then, poses a critical question to a contemporary theory of political order: Does there remain a place for the decision beyond law, or is our political life wholly ordered by law? Is such completeness precisely what we mean by a constitutional regime and the rule of law? Can we imagine the exception as anything other than a violation? If politics has become a domain wholly ordered by law, there is no need for a political theology. The point is analogous to religious theology: if all that is, or can be, is fully explained on the basis of physical laws, there is no room for theological inquiry. Traditionally, theology begins only with faith in the miraculous: the sovereign decision for creation. The miracle is the exception. It is moreover, an exception that requires a deci-sion. Thus, David Hume defines a miracle as a "transgression of a law of nature by a particular volitional act of the Diety."[2] Absent the volitional act—that is, the decision—the exception would appear not as miracu-lous but as arbitrary and chaotic. There is literally a world of difference between the miracle and the lawless. That difference is the presence of the sovereign decision. Similarly, a sovereign who could no longer decide for the miraculous would have become empty, a mere idol. Of such gods, we have no need, whether in metaphysics or politics. Rejecting the category of the sovereign, science knows no exceptions; it has only the category of the "not yet explained." A polity that rejects the concept of sovereignty will have only the categories of the legal and the illegal.

SOVEREIGN AND EXCEPTION

A legal order can be viewed abstractly as a system of norms in which every norm is related to all of the others. Those relationships can be hier-archical or horizontal. The former grounds the place of deduction in legal reasoning; the latter grounds the place of analogy. Together, these two kinds of relationships mean that the entire legal order is on view from every point in the whole. Every norm gives us access to the entire legal world. In this sense, law is like a language.[3] Standing within such a system, one never gets beyond it. Thus, of every proposed action, we can ask, "Is it legal?" We answer that question through a combination of deductive and analogical reasoning.[4] If we were bound in all of our political perceptions to see the world through the frame of law, we would never get to the exception.

We are not so bound. Legal norms enter our lived experience tied to other forms of meaning, including other understandings of politics. To say that law is a complete system of order is not to say that it is exclu-sive. Instead, it is like saying that there is no experience of which we cannot give a scientific account. That proposition hardly rules out aes-thetic or moral accounts. Describing the cause of an event will not tell us whether we judge it to be beautiful. Two such positions "outside" of the legal norms are equity and revolution. Equity reveals, on the smallest scale, this possibility of political decisions evoking meanings set against the ordinary legal norm. Revolution—a paradigmatic instance of the Schmittian exception—does so on the largest scale. While they differ dramatically in scale, both constitute exceptions, and both require a decision. They are linked to each other as the miracle of creation is linked to the miraculous answer to a singular prayer.

Equity and revolution are outside of law but not illegal. They mark the point at which judgments of legality lose their hold on the imagination. Even though both equity and revolution make reference to law—both hold forth law as the norm—neither is an application of law. The norm, Schmitt often says, requires ordinary circumstances for its operation; the exception occupies those circumstances that are less— or more—than ordinary. The quality of the exception is always one of self-limitation: the exception cannot become normal.[5] Nevertheless, the nature of norms is such that the exception is always subject to normalization: law will seek to extend to the exceptional decision.

Schmitt does not say that the sovereign is only present in the decision for the exception, and such a view would not be plausible. Surely sovereignty is at stake in the rule of law as well as in the exception. Historically, we see that the judicial writ of authority formally issued from the king; the judge spoke in the name of the king.[6] Again, the theological analogy can serve us: from the belief that God has the power of miraculous intervention, it hardly follows that the ordinary workings of nature do not equally reflect His creative act. Indeed, precisely because nature is the product of His free act, it remains open to the possibility of a new demonstration of that freedom.[7] Sovereignty is not the alternative to law, but the point at which law and exception intersect—at stake in both is the free act. The historical and theological connection is also evident as a matter of logic: there can be no exception without reference to a norm. Without that reference, the exception becomes mere anarchy: not the miraculous intervention, but law's failure. The miracle must affirm the norm, at the same time that it violates the norm. Accordingly, a conception of the sovereign that begins from the exception cannot help but affirm the norm as well. Only a deliberate act—a conscious choice—can have these simultaneous qualities of affirmation and negation.

While the exception must include a reference to the norm, does the norm necessarily include a reference to the exception? Can we imagine a world without exception—that is, one that is fully "normalized"? Of course we can. That is the worldview of the natural sciences, on the one hand, and of bureaucratic rationality, on the other. What we cannot easily imagine is the possibility of freedom in a world that is fully normalized. This was exactly the problem with which Kant struggled: how, in a law-governed world, to preserve a place for freedom that is not arbitrary. His answer too looked toward sovereign creation: a free act must be one in which the subject gives the law to himself. A free order, Schmitt responds, is one in which the exception is possible. The exception represents the possibility of free choice, and choice requires a subject—the sovereign—who decides. In the Schmittian exception, for just this reason, the norm itself is the object of choice—not, however, as in Kant's giving a rule to oneself. Rather, it is that for the sake of which a decision is made. The inversion here is critical: the norm does not determine the decision; rather the decision is for the norm. The sovereign must affirm the norm in a world in which he can will the exception. If the political order is to be understood as the product of freedom, then rule and exception must each imply the other.

SOVEREIGN POWER TO DECIDE: EQUITY

Schmitt introduces the exception "as a case of extreme peril"—he is thinking of an existential threat to the state. But we do better to start on a smaller scale. The contrast of law and exception, of judge and sovereign, restates at a higher level the traditional contrast of law and equity. Equity embodied the idea that there must be the possibility of exceptions to a legal rule. Without such a possibility, justice—the assumed goal of all legal norms—would fail. The point is as at least as old as Aristotle.[8] The puzzle is how to do justice while violating just norms. Were the norm itself unjust, the right response would be to reform the law. Equity creates the exception while affirming the norm.

The English system of equity also linked the exception to the sovereign. The common-law courts applied the norm; speaking in his name, they were the mediated voice of the king. The immediate presence of the king, however, was located in the Chancery and the Star Chamber—the civil and criminal sites of equity. These panels were frequently described as "keeping the king's conscience." His presence was an aspect of their physical structure even if he did not always actually participate.[9] Exercising the power to decide on exceptions to norms was not just a matter of administration. Rather, the panel relied directly on the king's sacral character, which in this regard had a double aspect: in part, it was a matter of fulfilling his Christian obligation to do good; in part, it was a matter of displaying his own will as the site of ultimate meaning in the state.[10] Absent the sacral presence, the exception could look like nothing more than a failure of law, that is, as an instance of injustice. While justice under law is a function of reason, the exception is a matter of presence.

We only capture part of the problem here if we ground it in the complexity of human circumstances, noting that no rule can capture all of that diversity. This might be true, but it models the equitable decision as a further—now *ad hoc*—application of the rule, which must be refined to deal with particular circumstances: a better rule or rules would pick up more of this complexity. God's love, however, responds to particulars not because his reason is inadequate, but because justice without love is inadequate. God's goodness is always both universal and particular—or why else would there be prayer? His justice is never separate from His love. If it were to become so, vengeance would be both terrible and endless. If the king's end was to achieve God's ends on earth, then political institutions had to achieve some kind of synthesis of the universal and the particular, of justice and love, of rule and exception. A sacral monarch was as much a loving parent as an instrument of justice. Thus, King James described the role of Chancery as "mixing Mercy with Justice, where other Courts proceed only according to strict rules of law."[11]

It is much more difficult for us today to understand the character of the legal exception as something other than a violation of the norm. It has the air of partiality about it: not love, but interest. Norms specify behavior that has been abstracted from the person who is doing the acting. Justice, we say, treats like cases alike. By "like," we refer to similarly situated individuals, not to their character. The exception, understood as an opening for love and mercy, is directed at the person as a unique subject. We need justice and love because we are always both one of many and uniquely a self. We hear still an echo of this idea in the often repeated phrase in periods of democratic transition that we must "forgive the person, not the crime."

Who, however, is to exercise love over justice once we have detached sovereignty from personhood? To temper justice with love is a virtue of character; it is, accordingly, a difficult virtue to attach to an institution.[12] Only with some difficulty can we ask for love from an institution. Were courts responsive in this direction, for example, we would more likely speak of a failure of law—and of justice—then of justice tempered by mercy. The perception of partiality in the exception was not such a problem in the premodern era, for the sacral monarch embodied the double character of universal and particular. Exactly this double character made him Christlike.

The sacral monarch expressed the miraculous as the presence of the infinite in the finite in at least three respects: first, in the king's two bodies; second, in the practice of curing the sick through a laying on of hands; and third, through the exercise of equity.[13] These were all interrelated. A king who could cure the body outside the laws of nature could also cure social pathology outside of the laws of the realm. We see in the relationship of the macrostructure to the microdecision the ground of Schmitt's claim: "The existence of the state is undoubted proof of its superiority over the validity of the legal norm" (12). Before there could be any law at all, there had to be the king's body as the mystical corpus of the state. That was the sacred source, which could invest in and withdraw from particular finite formations. Existence before justice.

The exception might be exercised by man, but it rested on the sacred acting through man. Accordingly, the king placed on the bench of the equity chambers religious figures of authority.[14] Shakespeare speaks to this same tradition when he writes that "[mercy] is enthroned in the hearts of kings / It is an attribute of God himself; / An earthly power doth then show likest God's / When mercy seasons justice."[15] The exception that is beyond justice but not unjust is not human at all; it overflows with the presence of the sacred. The democratic version of this is

Lincoln's plea for "charity for all" in response to the suffering brought on by a God whose "judgments . . . are true and righteous altogether."[16] There is a familial side to this phenomenon as well: for love of family, I will make exceptions to a norm that I fully acknowledge to be just.

At issue in the crown's equity powers, then, was the being of the sacral monarch—one who opened a space for the sacred in and through his very presence. Standing in the place of Christ, the sovereign had to be able to will the exception, which is the miraculous presence that can stand outside of law without appearing partial or arbitrary. To be exempt from law was to be marked—the idea goes all the way back to Cain.[17] The moral value of he who bears the exception is always ambiguous: unjust and loved, polluted and sacred.[18]

In our secular age, an echo of the sacral presence of the king is still found in the pardon power. This is a remnant of the sovereign power to decide on the exception to the law. It always verges on lawlessness as we try to find a ground for mercy that does not appear to be mere partiality. That ground can only be care, which is always personal and unbound by rules. We may feel that we need a pardon power; yet, if we cannot speak of care, love, or the sacred, we are at a loss to offer a justification that is consistent with our other beliefs about the rule of law. Our ordinary inclination, then, is to displace pardon by a system of "earned probation," administered by a bureaucratic board. We seek to normalize the exception.

When we assign the pardon power to the chief executive, we worry that we are putting him above the law: where is justice outside of law? Yet when Grant Gilmore writes, "In Hell, there will be nothing but law," we understand his point.[19] The pardon power still has something of the character of the laying on of hands, of the mark of the sacred, indeed of the blessing. It is not quite the same as an act of forgiveness, for there is no need for the beneficiary even to admit guilt. The pardon is always undeserved. It literally takes the bearer outside of law. It is a gift that comes as if from nowhere. Indeed, if we can give an account of its exercise in a particular case—that is, if we can offer a causal explanation of how the pardon came to be granted—we are more likely to judge it corrupt.[20]

SOVEREIGN POWER TO DECIDE: THE BORDERLINE

Equity and pardon point to a need to act freely beyond law. Both had their origins in the free act of the sacral-monarch. With the disappearance of that concept, both have become problematic. Pardon has just barely survived; equity jurisdiction has long since been fused with the ordinary jurisdiction of courts of law.[21] Ours is an age in which deviation from the norm is suspect: no one creates a power to decide for the exception behind the Rawlsian veil of ignorance. The whole point of that veil is to subordinate will to reason, the particular to the universal.

Reflection on equity, nevertheless, points us in the right direction for thinking about the political limits of a legal norm. To advance further we must slightly modify Schmitt's definition of the sovereign to make it accessible to modern sensibilities: "Sovereign power is that of deciding on the exception." We must, in other words, depersonalize the sovereign. Once we are outside of the tradition of equity and individual care, there is no particular reason to think that such a power must be exercised by a natural person, as opposed to a collective agent or an institution. For Americans, Schmitt's reference to a single subject as sovereign is likely to seem to point in the direction of the president—an unacceptable proposition. Because of our tradition of opposition to anything that looks like monarchical power, most presidential claims for exceptional powers of decision come with historical baggage that clouds the inquiry into fundamental theory.[22]

The location of sovereign power is not an issue of definition but of the functioning of an actual political organization. That locus is not necessarily stable; it can shift as a result of contest or, conversely, of desuetude. A god that fails to act—to demonstrate its miraculous power—will lose that power, for it has no power outside of the community's faith, and an unexercised faith is no faith at all. Sovereign power does not exist as an institution's or person's potential; rather, it exists only in the act of decision itself. At best, a definition can tell us what we should be looking for; a scheme of government can tell us where we might look. "The most guidance the constitution can provide is to indicate who can act in such a case" (7). The scheme cannot tell us, however, what we will find at the moment of decision. What we will see depends most of all on what we are prepared to see. An exceptional act offered in care can be received as nothing more than a transgression of a just norm.

A constitution's attempt to establish the locus of sovereign power may not successfully identify the actual sovereign in the concrete situation. Louis XVI may have thought he could exercise sovereign power; he may have had the "constitutional" authority to exercise such power. When he decided on the exception, however, no one responded—or, at least, insufficient numbers responded to bring about the political event. Faith in his sovereign authority had failed and, with that, he lost his sacred character. Where once people had seen the presence of divine power, they now saw only a sad and somewhat lost individual with no power whatsoever. He had become Citizen Louis Capet who would be the victim of some other sovereign's decision.

The democratic revolutions that displaced Europe's sacral-monarchs had the quality of dispersing the claim to sovereign power. That power could now appear anywhere and thus everywhere. What mattered was the exercise of the decision and the community's perception of the sovereign will at that point of decision, whether in the streets of Paris or on the common of Lexington. With dispersion of the sovereign power, however, the traditional foundation of the equity and the pardon powers is disturbed. A dispersed sovereign can more easily act for revolution than it can act for the benefit of the particular individual. The closest thing we have today to the sacral-monarch's power to create the exception to law may not be the executive pardon but jury nullification, which is best seen as a localized expression of the popular sovereign willing the exception.[23]

In political organizations, as in individual life, a decision with no effect is not a decision. It is a gesture, perhaps a symbol of lost power. To intervene in the world requires an act, not merely an idea or deliberation. The sovereign power is not that of recognizing or identifying the exception; it is the power to decide on the exception. It requires will, not reason. As with every phenomenon of the will, it has no essence apart from its existence. It makes no sense to say that sovereign power should be at one locus rather than another or that it should be exercised in one situation rather than another.[24] There are no norms that can get us from an idea to an exception, whether we are talking about the self or the polity. Within a legal order there is always a "should." About the exception there is only the decision in the concrete situation. Unlike reason, there is no will in the abstract.

A constitutional order may attempt to identify the sovereign, as in the French Salic Law.[25] A modern, liberal constitution, however, is more likely to deny that sovereign power is localized anywhere in the state: "All tendencies of modern constitutional development point toward eliminating the sovereign in this sense" (7). Immediately, however, Schmitt responds that "whether the extreme exception can be banished from the world is not a juristic question" (7). We cannot make the world over by a theory. The exception cannot be banished from our experience by virtue of a theoretical scheme that leaves no place for it, even when that scheme is put in place in a formal constitution. To think that possible is like thinking that justice can banish love or that law can do without mercy. Even if we honestly believe that our political life has progressed to the point at which legal norms are adequate to resolve every concrete situation of conflict, the belief that this will continue to be the case must appeal to what Schmitt calls "philosophical-historical or metaphysical convictions" (7). Whether such convictions are an accurate characterization of the polity can only be known in the concrete situation. We know sovereignty exists when we see it operate. That operation may take the form of war or the form of mercy. Both are exceptions to law; both rely on will over reason, on love over justice. Both remind us that the God of the West has always been both just and loving.

Until the exceptional situation, our "metaphysical convictions" are only speculations. That speculation, of course, can be more or less informed by history. History tells us that politics—the life of a nation—is not likely to take the form that a normative theory demands. It is not too much to say that the exception has been at least as important as the rule in the history of the Western nation-state.[26] Nevertheless, the modern rule of law does not see the exception as a necessary supplement but as failure and violation.[27] A modern constitution will attempt to constrain the possibility of the exception by disabling the claim to sovereign authority: "the liberal constitutional state . . . attempts to repress the question of sovereignty by a division and mutual control of competencies" (11). Such efforts, however, may do no more than push off the boundary of the exception.

That boundary is not marked simply by the appearance of the unusual. Much that is of an irregular nature happens in the daily life of the polity. The exception is not the unusual, the difficult, or even the stressful. Schmitt writes that the exception is "not merely . . . a construct applied to any emergency decree or state of siege" (6). Political life is often unpredictable and dangerous. Political actors must have the competence to deal with the unexpected. That competence is what we commonly call "discretion." Discretion, however, is subject to judicial evaluation under norms. The court asks whether the decision was "reasonable," whether it was reached in a procedurally fair fashion, and whether it stayed within the established jurisdictional boundaries.

Such discretionary judgments are not new with the rise of the administrative state. Judgment necessarily attaches to governance; it is still judgment in the application of a norm. When the doctor prescribes an exception to the normal course of treatment, he is not opening a space for the miraculous. He is further specifying the rule in this situation of the concrete particular. The same sort of professional expertise was evident in the development of the common law, which advanced by distinguishing exceptions from general principles. No principle of law comes without a doctrine of "exceptions." These exceptions, unlike the Schmittian exception, do not stand on the sacral-power to act outside of law. They are rather points in the process of the specification and elaboration of law. Eventually, these exceptions are organized into a competing or complementary norm.

Conceptually, the norm must precede the exception. A world constituted only by exceptions would be one in which nothing followed from anything else.[28] We make sense of the world by applying norms, including laws, principles, and concepts. We organize experience under norms. Sometimes those norms take the form of rules, sometimes of standards. This does not mean that there are not difficult cases that don't quite fit under our understanding of the norms.[29] There are always things or events that we cannot easily place. We might argue over them; individuals might offer different interpretations. When two judges disagree on the proper outcome of a case, neither appeals to the exception. Rather, they are disagreeing over the meaning of the legal norm.[30] None of these difficult cases are exceptions in Schmitt's sense of a "borderline concept" (5). The border is that between a legal order, on the one hand, and chaos, on the other. If the exception falls off that line, it disappears into law or chaos. The exception absorbed by law is discretion; the exception absorbed by chaos is mere violence.

The sovereign decision for the exception continues into the present the story of the state's emergence—the first "emergency"—from the state of nature. The state of nature as threat never disappears but is only pushed out beyond the boundaries of the state. The state maintains itself as a presence in the world by keeping secure this line between itself and the chaotic state of nature. Classically, the realist in international relations gave a vivid representation of this borderline concept when he contrasted the settled political order within the territory of the state with the state of nature that continued outside of the border.[31] On the Hobbesian view, states have never entered into any relationship of subordination to a common power—the sovereign—that is the necessary condition of leaving the state of nature. Every state, accordingly, maintains a wary relationship to every other, always determining its behavior through a prudential calculus that may make reference to norms but is not committed to the norms independently of its own continued existence.

As long as the threatened exception is a strongly felt presence among states, there will be skepticism about whether international law is law. In turn, there will be a reluctance of states to submit their disputes to institutions of judicial authority.[32] Israel, for example, is not about to rely upon a court to decide on its claims to Jerusalem. Of course, some states might choose to do so, based upon particular, prudential judgments. But states do not submit the question of their own continued existence to adjudication. National existence is not about norms but will. When contemporary international lawyers argue that a state committing gross violations of international human rights norms forfeits, as a legal matter, its sovereign claim against nonintervention, they are arguing the opposite:

norms are now a condition of existence.[33] Of course, this position is arguably counter to the U.N. Charter itself, which does not condition the right of self-defense on compliance with any norms of internal governance.[34]

To describe the exception as a "borderline" concept is to imagine the state of nature, which is ordinarily pushed out beyond the boundaries of the state, breaching those boundaries. The Schmittian exception appears whenever the existence of the state as an organized, historical presence is threatened. It is the crisis triggered by the threatened collapse of those institutions that sustain the borders. Those borders are both literal, as when the state suffers an invasion, and metaphorical, as when the threat to the ordinary order arises from within. Internal threats leading to the decision for the exception can arise from political violence (for example, civil war) but also from natural disturbance (disease, drought, hurricanes) and social crisis. In all such cases, "the state suspends the law in the exception on the basis of its right of self-preservation" (12).

In cases of both external and internal threat, what is really at stake is the character of the polity as a certain kind of order. If one did not think that existence in this sense was at stake, there would be no reason to defend the state. There would be no "ordinary" against which and for the sake of which to decide upon the exception. If one can be one thing just as easily as another, there can be no threat to existence. In politics, there is no line to be drawn between identity and existence. The state's identity is its existence. The state is not a mere collection of individuals or a geographic setting. It is defined by its constitution, not necessarily a written document but the actual organization of the polity as of a certain sort. This is the Aristotelian formal cause of the polity; it makes it one thing and not another. This is the sense in which a revolution can pose the same threat to the state as an external attack. If the attack takes the form of humanitarian intervention and the revolution that of a fascist coup, we might have good reason to value the first more than the second. The point, however, is not to make normative judgments but to understand the "exception," which is an analytic, not an evaluative, concept. The sovereign power to decide upon the exception is the power to identify the event—from whatever source—that is a threat to the state as a particular organization of political life.

The exception is precisely not a situation that satisfies a definition or a set of conditions. It is an existential concept. We cannot know in advance from where the threat to the existence of the political order will come. We cannot even be sure that any particular event poses such a threat: if we could know, we could subject the situation to a norm. There can be no juridical norm by which to measure the exception, not just because the exception is "unpredictable," but because there can be no norm without the possibility of error. A legal order recognizes the possibility of error in its doctrines of appellate review, of reversal of precedent, and of amendment. We cannot, however, describe the exception as right or wrong. At the micro level, we cannot say that an exercise—or a withholding—of mercy was an error. The quality of mercy may be wise or unwise but not because it applies a norm. At the macro level, the exception depends upon a perception of threat. At stake is the imagination, not the facts of the matter. Again, it can be unwise, but there is no measure of error outside of the political imagination of the community. Once the sovereign decides on the exception, we cannot know what might otherwise have happened. What we cannot know, we cannot measure.

The exception, accordingly, can only be recognized in the decision. More precisely, it is constituted in the decision itself. The truth of the matter is not something apart from the decision. Having decided, the sovereign has brought the exception into existence. Conversely, without the exception, there is no sovereign presence. Exactly what political role would be left for a sovereign in a state in which the entire character of politics was comprehended within a system of norms and their application? Even lawmaking would become a function of following legally specified procedures: it would be progress in the articulation of existing law, not the revolutionary rule of creating the new and destroying the old.

In our contemporary world, relationships among states are increasingly thought to be regulated by an alternative legal regime—international law. Together international and domestic law are to subject the entire domain of the political to juridification. Reflecting this project of universal juridification, we increasingly find assertions that the very idea of sovereign power is anachronistic.[35] Schmitt's opening sentence, then, expresses a vision to which our world may be becoming the counterpoint. Political theology begins with recognition that the power to decide upon the exception is constitutive of sovereignty. Conversely, "no exception, no sovereignty" might serve as the motto of those enamored with the globalization of the rule of law today.

SOVEREIGNTY AND THE DECISION

Situated in a modern political order, first of all and most of the time we see that world in and through law. Nevertheless, at the borders of our imagination stand concepts of beginnings and ends, of revolution and capitulation. We understand that our legal order had a beginning and we acknowledge that it will have an end. Law inhabits the time in-between.[36] Earlier generations believed that if the political order could be aligned with the cosmological order, there was no reason to believe that it would inevitably fail in the course of human history. Today, we are deeply historicized. Political order, we believe, ends well short of Judgment Day.

Aware of this in-between character, the legal consciousness always has a sense of its own boundedness, that is, of its own limits. These limits are both temporal and spatial. We live within our political order as one possibility among a range of possibilities. We know ourselves as entirely contingent, the product not of God's act but of acts taken—or not taken—on a human scale. We see the political order within a temporal framework in the same way that we see ourselves as individuals. Each of us is bound to our own imagination, but each understands the bounded character of that imagination. We see the extraordinary character of our own beginning and end. To raise those endpoints to reflective consciousness is to take a step toward the theological, for it is to theorize that which we cannot actually experience. From the standpoint of our ordinary experience, beginning and end are both absolutely exceptional and absolutely necessary.

Americans—apart from the experience of the Confederacy—have not had to think much of capitulation, but they have never abandoned the idea of themselves as the inheritors of revolution. They intuitively understand that law is a product of revolution. Law and revolution together constitute the frame of our political imaginary. Revolution tells us that the entire legal order arises from a moment of sovereign decision. This is the sense in which the exception is tied to law but is not itself subject to law. Of such exceptional moments, Schmitt says they reveal the decision in its "absolute purity," by which he means a decision ungrounded in any preexistent norm (13). There is no measuring the truth of revolution by any other political norm. A successful revolution establishes its own value by creating its own truth. An unsuccessful revolution loses the right even to claim the title of "revolution." It is not an exception but only a moment for the application of the law; it is politics as criminal act.[37] The absolute purity of the sovereign decision for revolution is located exactly in this existential claim: existence precedes essence. At this moment, there is nothing but the sovereign will to decide.

Revolution, as the paradigmatic exception, is always both a negative and a positive phenomenon. It negates the ordinary character of the status quo. If that were all, however, it would be the cataclysm that returns a polity to the state of nature. Revolution is more than that because it is a creative force. It brings forth an order of law as the will of the popular sovereign. That a polity is of one sort rather than another is based on nothing more than the sovereign decision. A polity makes itself by deciding for a constitutional order: "Like every other order, the legal order rests on a decision and not on a norm" (10). Constitution is not just the product of revolution; it is the inner truth of revolution. But conversely—and equally—the revolutionary exception is the inner truth of constitution.

Once we take up the perspective of contingency, then norm and exception are inextricably bound to each other. Only as a matter of logic does the norm have priority over the exception. If history is contingency—not necessity—then norm is a function of decision. This is exactly what contingency means, that all order depends upon the exception. Postmodern thought puts the awareness of contingency at its center. It is hardly surprising, therefore, to see a recovery of Schmitt, despite his illiberal politics.

From within the legal frame, one law can only come from another. Describing the origin of a law, we say that the legislature produced it according to constitutionally specified procedures. This is the form of reasoning of the judicial opinion or, for that matter, of any argument made to a court. The lawyer does not say the farmers' lobby or the financial sector produced the law. The politics that accounts for law disappears from view; instead, we look to the secondary rules of a legal system that specify the procedure by which law is made. In this direction, we find the jurisprudence of Hans Kelsen, who insisted that a norm can only come from a norm because an "is" cannot produce an "ought."[38] We stumble immediately into the same metaphysical problem that so troubled Hume: since we can give a positive account of every event in the world (the farmers' lobby), how does the normative arise? Kelsen offered the same sort of transcendental answer as Kant: there must be a ground-norm as the source of all that is normative, for the divide between the is and the ought is unbridgeable. Such a superior norm is the transcendental condition of law.

Political theology gives a different sort of answer. It understands authority as decision, links decision to sovereign, and grounds sovereignty in faith. At the foundation is not yet another norm—the ground-norm—but the decision, which always cuts across the is and the ought.[39] It *is* the decision for the *norm*. The moment of will grounds reason. This point echoes, to some degree, Austin's claim that law is grounded in the sanction, not the norm. But "sanction" is the wrong way to grasp the expression of the will that is the decision. It is only an external sign of the decision. Similarly, it substitutes fear (fear of the sanction) for faith (faith in the sovereign).

Norms remain lifeless absent the decision. To insist on the place of decision and exception in the political order is to find common ground with the theologian of creation and the modern existentialist. In the lived world of the law, the decision is just as important as the norm, which means that faith is as important as justice. The leap of faith grounds the norm. Not surprisingly, Schmitt concludes chapter one with a long quotation from Kierkegaard, ending with the line: "The exception . . . thinks the general with intense passion" (15). We cannot have reason without will, because no matter how just the norms, they do not become norms for us until we will their existence.

We know what the norm disengaged from the decision looks like: an abstract generality found in the law books or a theory alongside other theories. But what does the decision look like disengaged from the norm? It cannot be merely arbitrary action, despite Kierkegaard's dictum that "the moment of decision is madness."[40] In an arbitrary world, there is no difference between a decision and a failure to decide. Nothing is at stake because nothing is invested in one outcome over others. For this reason, a world in which decision is arbitrary cannot be distinguished from a world in which everything is determined. Neither is it a world of freedom. This was Kant's insight: a world of will without norms is a world governed by external causes. The explanations we would point to in such a world would not refer to the subject's decision but to the external influences upon the subject. It would be heteronomy, not autonomy. Outside of the freely determined act, there is only a causal sequence. We need then to grasp the idea of a decision that is not determined by a norm but that is also not arbitrary with respect to the norm.

This mysterious relationship of decision to norm is revealed in the exception, which is never a moment under the norm but which is nonsensical without reference to the norm. "Order," Schmidt writes, "in the juristic sense still prevails even if it is not of the ordinary kind" (12). It is not ordinary because in no sense is it a product of application of the norm. Because the decision is not an instance of the rule, we might call it a "singular." This hardly means, however, that the decision on the exception is either arbitrary or causally determined. From the political point of view, arbitrariness and causality would both constitute "anarchy and chaos," which is precisely not a manifestation of sovereign authority to decide. Just the opposite: the decision holds off anarchy and chaos. The threat of revolution will always be seen by those who exercise authority under existing law as the threat of chaos. Once the revolution comes to be seen as the sovereign decision, however, it becomes the source of order against such threats of chaos. To defend the state as a legal order is to defend the revolutionary inheritance.

At issue in the sovereign decision at the moment of the Schmittian exception is not the application of a particular norm but the entire legal order. The sovereign decision at that point exists for the sake of the entire system. The sovereign decides outside of law for the sake of law. The sovereign decision, accordingly, is the act of the state willing its own existence. "The state suspends the law in the exception on the basis of its right of self-preservation" (12). When we ask what is the content of the self that is affirmed in the exception, we begin the process of specifying the content of law. The sovereign wills itself into existence; it will be what it wills itself to be. The end of the exception, accordingly, is always to overcome itself. It is to reestablish the ordinary conditions of existence within which norms can operate through judgments.[41]

We might use an analogy from contemporary physics to express this: the sovereign decision for the exception is the big bang that contains the entire order of the universe in its potential form. That singular moment is uncaused; there is no time from which it is causally derived. It is, nevertheless, not an expression of chaos. It is the uncaused cause of the whole; we have no other point of access to the big bang except from the universe that follows. Because we can see it only from the point of view of its realization, the point at which potential has already moved to actual, we cannot judge it as arbitrary. Just the opposite: it is the one thing that is truly necessary, if there is to be anything at all. Before the big bang, there was no truth; all truth is a product of the event.

Schmitt does not have this cosmological idea available to him, but he does have its theological equivalent: creation. Reading the Biblical account, one has a God's-eye view on creation. Seeing the darkness over the deep, one imagines the sovereign decision as uncaused and thus literally coming from nowhere.[42] Creation ex nihilo is the pure moment of decision. There is nothing from which we can derive, measure, or predict creation in the Old Testament story. We see it as contingent but not as just one possibility among others. We do not see God choosing from a variety of possible worlds and measuring their virtues against some abstract norm.[43] There is literally no text before creation. When God judges creation good, he is not comparing it to other worlds or appealing to some standard outside of the creative act. It is good because it is. His act contains all that is or can be. It is all present in that instant, for we can make no sense of time or space prior to that act. Accordingly, the power to decide for creation is also the power of omniscience: there simply is nothing else to know—at least until man becomes free.[44]

Schmitt follows a traditional line of theological thought by moving the creation myth—or at least his political version of it—deep into history itself. The theological question is, what sustains the created universe? Why does it not fall back into nothingness (a kind of premodern version of entropy)? The answer is that God's creative act does not occur only as a now-past, historical event. Rather, God's creative act fills all time. Thus, God's will sustains His created world. This is one meaning of God's grace. Were He to withdraw that grace, the universe would become once again what it was before the act: nothing at all. The decision for existence must be made at every moment.

Metaphysics and morality—the is and the ought—intersect here. One cannot believe in God's grace but be indifferent to the normative order willed in the act of grace. Everything that we are and all that we can be depend upon the grace of God. To be is to be sustained by the divine will. Free will is the capacity to act outside of the boundaries of that grace—the literal boundaries of Eden serve as a symbol of the bounded quality of grace. To be cast out is to be on our own, which means both to struggle to will the good and to face death. In the religious tradition, to pursue freedom outside of grace is to put death in the place of life; it is sin.[45] The Christological version of this thought, now in the form of the recovery of God's grace after the Fall, is that all existence is renewed in and through the body of Christ. God does not just create a world as an object apart from Himself. He wills it into being and it is only His will that sustains it in being. The body of Christ is the will of God made real in historical time. Thus, Christ can be described as pure decision for the exception. His is the sacrifice that makes possible the norm. Accordingly, Christ is essentially and completely that which we all are as a matter of metaphysical necessity.

All of these speculations—metaphysical and theological—point to what is at stake in the idea of the decision. The sovereign power is pure will. The sovereign must will the state into existence. In revolution, but also at the extreme moment of self-defense, we see that will in its "absolute purity." At that moment, the will contains in potential form all that the state is or may become. This is the sense in which the exception contains the rule but is not subject to the rule. We must not think of the state as something that simply happens in the world like a fact of nature. Neither, however, is it a mere order of norms derived from other norms. The state is not a thing or a rule; it is a power that is continually making history one way rather than another. It requires energy—*dunamis* in the classical sense. It must continually will itself into being. Absent that will, it may find itself simply brushed aside by other political organizations that assert themselves in the same space and time. This is true externally as states compete for presence and power but internally as well when different factions will their own conceptions of political order. The subject whose will would negate the state is the enemy. Accordingly, Schmitt places the distinction between friend and enemy at the foundation of "political actions and motives."[46]

In the competitive world of power, abstract norms don't count for much. There is always a surfeit of such norms. Everyone can have their own theory, even their own interpretation of existing norms. Justice as an abstraction founds no state. Consider the Universal Declaration of Human Rights, which expresses just norms but has no power to create political order. Every norm depends for its practical existence upon a decision. It must be taken up as the object of the will of some individual or group. Similarly, the entire system of norms—the state as a symbolic order—depends upon the decision, the sovereign decision.

Every legal order has some characteristic unity.[47] It has a systemic character that represents the elaboration of a certain characteristic self-understanding embodied ultimately in the individual participants in that legal order. That we live in one legal order rather than another cannot be the result of some set of super norms. It is, rather, as if we decided to create ourselves. We are the product of our own decision. We must conceive of our political order as the product of a free act—of a decision—if we are to understand politics as a product of the free will. That free act appears at the moment of origin and again at the moment of threat: it is implicitly present at every moment. The operative content of that decision must make reference to the norms conceived as a unity—we will ourselves to be something. But the act is never explained by the norms. Neither reason nor will alone but the interaction of both explains the human condition—including politics. Behind this concept of the sovereign is an idea of the freedom of the will in its political form. But for the exception, we might be well ordered but not free.

Sovereign power operates beyond law to create and to protect law. The character of the exception will reflect the legal order. This means that the exception is not some uniform condition that threatens every state equally: "[A] militaristic bureaucracy, a self-governing body controlled by the spirit of commercialism, or a radical party organization" will each find the threat to its existence in very different situations (9–10). Democratic theory has long stumbled over the conundrum of the possibility of democratic politics producing nondemocratic outcomes. Schmitt's idea of the sovereign exception would operate at this point were such an outcome threatened.[48] When who we are is thrown into issue, the question is what we will do. We learn who we are by learning where we stand and what we stand for. Just here, at the moment of the exception that calls forth the decision, or the decision that determines the exception, existence determines essence.

Just as the application of a legal norm can be perverted through an abuse of power, so can the sovereign decision. This was recognized already in classical political theory: the moment at which the king becomes a tyrant. Perhaps the claim of sovereign power is particularly subject to such abuse since, by definition, it is not subject to a juridical norm and there is no institutionalized mechanism of review. Surely, many kings became tyrants. There is, however, nothing in the theory of the exception that counsels against a legal order establishing mechanisms of review for the actual decisions made by an executive—or anyone else. The chief executive might declare an exception and find himself impeached. If he is successfully held to account, the exception was not present and sovereign power has not been exercised. Here, we might think of Truman's seizure of the steel mills during the Korean War. That was not a sovereign decision for the exception. It was not because it was reviewed by the Supreme Court and settled by the application of legal norms.[49] Not even the dissenters believed Truman's act to be an exception. Just the opposite: they thought his behavior fit within the execution of existing legal norms. We cannot know in advance where law might end. Theory can only say that as long as the exception is imagined as a possibility, the sovereign power is imagined as a political necessity.

LAW WITHOUT SOVEREIGNTY?

In beginning the text with the exception rather than the norm, Schmitt was battling against the current of modern, jurisprudential thought. What had been an issue primarily of theory when he was writing—often with Kelsen as his target—has become a deeper set of political and cultural beliefs today. His was still a world in which one could speak of the sovereign as a "he." The Weimar Constitution allowed the President to declare an exception: Hitler stepped into this exceptional space. Other European leaders too filled such a space, for example, Mussolini. As the locus of the sovereign decision, they were not so different from the sacral-monarchs who had preceded them. Not so today. By the end of the twentieth century, not only had we depersonalized the sovereign, but the West had taken a decisive turn toward the rule of law as the single source of political order. A modern constitution imagines no political situation or action to which the law does not apply; it can imagine nothing that cannot be evaluated as a matter of law.

Today, the answer to the question of when law recognizes its own suspension may be, as a formal matter, precisely never. Any derogation from the ordinary legal order must itself be lawfully regulated. This is exactly why the rest of the world has had such a negative reaction to the exceptional situation created by the Americans at Guantanamo, calling it a "legal black hole." It is also why the American Supreme Court slowly pushed the situation there toward normalization.[50] This exception is to be subject to legal standards of procedure and substance—standards applied in a process of judicial review. The Court must say this—on this turns its own understanding of the rule of law—although it is in no hurry to say this, which is a way of allowing the exception to govern the emergency.[51]

This insistence on normalization as juridification, however, does not mean that the exception is impossible any more than it means that revolution is not possible. It means only that the exception is a legally "noncognizable" event, a point we have always known about revolution. An event is lawful when it is understood as the realization of a possibility already established by a prior law. It is, in other words, understood as an instance of a rule. The exception is exactly that which does not stand under any rule. It exists only as act, not as potential; as instance, not as rule. If it comes to be, it will always surprise us.

When Schmitt was writing, he was looking at the character of liberal, constitutional jurisprudence as it was coming to dominate the order of European states: "The tendency of liberal constitutionalism to regulate the exception as precisely as possible means, after all, the attempt to spell out in detail the case in which law suspends itself" (14). Today, a compelling example of juridification of the exception is found in transnational law. For example, under Article 15 of the European Convention of Human Rights, a state may issue a declaration of derogation with respect to some rights but not others. That decision, however, is always subject to judicial review. It can, as a legal matter, be right or wrong.[52] This is the juridical version of the exception, which is not an exception at all but only the invocation of another rule.

That a derogation decision can be subject to judicial review hardly means that the political order is deficient in failing to recognize the possibility of an exception. That absence is neither a virtue nor a vice; it is not a moral issue at all. What it means is that the political entity is not, in this respect, sovereign. It is a legal order without sovereignty. Often, we want law without sovereignty. This is, for example, exactly what the European Union is and perhaps we are all the better for that. To put this more directly: the European Union has no capacity to defend itself, if its existence were to come under threat either externally or internally. But there is no reason to think that it should have such a capacity.

If we were to stop here, we might think that the exception has become irrelevant to the modern legal order. But why would we think that the European legal order, particularly the Strasbourg order, is one of infinite duration? Like any other political construction, at some point its authority will be denied. What happens then? Of course, the existing mechanisms of enforcement may be adequate to bring the system back into order. A legal order hardly faces an exception whenever there is non-compliance. But we would be either naive or presumptuous to think that there could never be a moment at which existing mechanisms prove to be inadequate to that task. At the point at which there is nothing more to be done, the system may simply break apart or readjust to a smaller scheme of complying members. This is what it means to be a legal order without sovereignty. Of those political entities that withdraw, however, we would likely find ourselves again using the language of sovereignty to describe what was at issue.

It may well be the case—indeed, it is likely—that our regimes of international law and our transnational legal institutions will continue to operate without sovereignty. There is no sovereign power in the United Nations; it has no capacity to protect the order of international law from an existential threat to its own existence. Its dissolution is unlikely to lead to a civil war among factions making competing claims to speak in the voice of a global sovereign. States may find participation in their interests, but they do not define friends and enemies in terms of this institution. This is an empirical observation, not a normative judgment. It is contingent and could become otherwise.

Most normative orders operate without sovereign power: think of the order of a corporation, a church, or a university. The mistake is to think that law without sovereignty—in particular, international law—has solved the problem of perpetuating its own existence. The present form of this idea is that "networks" are themselves self-perpetuating.[53] If we think that the present order of law will simply continue indefinitely, changed only by processes internal to the legal order itself, then we are neither observing nor judging. Rather, we are indulging what Schmitt called a "philosophical-anthropological" or a "metaphysical" assumption. We might express that assumption as "the end of history" or the perfection of man.[54] It is simultaneously a deeply optimistic vision of the triumph of reason and a deeply pessimistic vision of the end of politics as a form of freedom. It misses something profound in the biblical story of the Fall: the Fall is both a condition and consequence of human freedom. To think of politics as the progressive realization of reason in the lawful ordering of human relations is an Enlightenment ideal based on a philosophical anthropology that begins and ends with reason.

The rule of reason has stepped into the place of the traditional appeal to "civilization" as the condition of participation in international law. Accordingly, even as the concept of natural law has fallen from favor, the element of consent has become less and less important in understanding the legitimacy of international law—consider, for example, the increasingly frequent appeals to allegedly *jus cogens* norms. But what about modern states? Have states themselves come to the point where they would no longer exercise sovereign power to protect themselves as self-sustaining legal orders? Have they too turned decisively from will to reason? After all, from the perspective of reason alone, there is not necessarily cause to defend one set of borders against another. Is jurisdiction simply a matter of convenience and efficiency once the substantive law of the state is understood to be the product of reason? Contemporary claims for universal jurisdiction rest on just such an understanding.

Schmitt has a vivid image in mind of the state that no longer rests on the sovereign will: that state that will not defend itself when attacked. Such a state may have a legal order in the ordinary sense: there are norms and judicial institutions. Nevertheless, at the moment of crisis, it simply declines to defend its own self-ordering as an existential value. At that point, the existence of the state as an organized entity with a jurisdictional reach and a continuous history—that is, as a force in the world— will come to an end. Perhaps this is how we should think of the demise of the Soviet Union: there was simply no power that could declare the exception in the defense of the state. Accordingly, it gave way to other entities that had such a power to make themselves in the world. The pressure that comes from within, pressing outward to sustain self-existence, is the presence of sovereignty.

Schmitt is at some distance from us in thinking that the pressure for self-existence applies as much to internal conflict as to external conflict. Ours, however, is a particularly Eurocentric view that has only lately arrived. If we consider the political struggles today in the Middle East or in Africa, we see just the sort of threat to the state's existence from civil war that Schmitt saw in post–World War I Europe. The source and direction of the threat is a function of history, not of theory. The challenge to a legal order as a self-sustaining system can arise through civil war as much as from external aggression. The sovereign decision is, accordingly, not always directed outward. If we only look outward, it is because our internal politics take place within a set of imaginative boundaries in which not all that much is at stake, that is, there are no revolutions on our horizons.

Americans can hardly claim that they are unfamiliar with this idea of internal conflict, for it captures what was at stake in our own Civil War. The nation did not act as if the resolution of the conflict was to be had through the application of a legal process. Regardless of what the Supreme Court may have thought in *Dred Scott*, it had no power to deploy law to resolve the conflict. Instead, that decision set the stage for the violent crisis. We need the language of sovereignty to describe the existential character of the stakes of such a conflict.

The Canadian Supreme Court has recently responded to the threat of Quebec's secession. It treated that threat as a possibility fully subject to a legal ordering.[55] It declined to see an existential threat against which the state must defend. The Canadian Court specified legal process as the way to reach a decision on Quebec. While the question might be unique in the Court's view, it hardly presented an exception to the legal order. Whether Canada continues as one unit or as two does not fundamentally matter because Quebec, were it to come into existence as a separate state, would certainly continue the liberal order of the rule of law. That is enough, if the state is imagined only as a means to individual well-being.

Nevertheless, we can no more take the Canadian Supreme Court's formulation of the issue as the truth of the matter than we could take the American Supreme Court's decision in *Dred Scott* as the truth of American pre–Civil War politics. Were Quebec to try to secede, we would only then learn of the shape and character of Canadian sovereignty. Unlike law, sovereign power does not exist as an abstraction. Its nature is only its existence. Until the decision, there is no such power; there is only speculation about what might be.

Not just the power to defend the legal order of the state but also the power to capitulate illustrates the concept of the sovereign. Indeed, this may be Schmitt's most interesting example of the exception. Who decides to declare defeat in a war? No legal/constitutional order extends to the situation of defeat. We cannot look to the constitution to discover who has this power to decide. Nor can there be judicial review of the decision to capitulate. To ask the question of capitulation is to confront the issue of the necessary conditions for the rule of law. Defeat is extraordinary, while law requires what Schmitt calls the "normal situation." Only from within the law does it seem that law creates the conditions of its own normality.

At the moment of defeat, there is no normal. There is no rule. There is only the decision. How is it made and by whom? The sovereign power to make this decision must be a power really to make it. It has no existence in form but only in fact. Either it is accomplished or it does not exist. If we imagine a president, king, or general signing instruments of capitulation but the defense of the state continued in fact, then we would have to say that there was no exercise of sovereign power. Sovereignty is never form without substance, because a failure of substance is an indication that a false claim has been made. This is just the sense in which sovereignty is an existential condition of the political; it is not a formal position within the legal order.

In this direction, of course, lies the real danger in Schmitt's thought. This is the danger of the populist dictator, the charismatic leader who decides by virtue of his claim to speak in the name of the people. What he says becomes the rule of action: the Fuhrer's word was the law. The danger is surely there, but the point is simply that a claim to sovereign power is no more true than the actual power to decide. The forms of sovereign power do not arrive from theory, but from the political culture. We cannot create a norm that eliminates the possibility of the rise of a charismatic leader, but we can practice forms of institutional politics that make it unlikely.

Whether someone or some group has such a power to decide is proven only in the concrete situation. A theory of sovereignty says nothing about who should have such a power. Indeed, the whole point of the theory of the exception is that there is no "should." Nor is it even the case that every imaginable legal order must locate a point of sovereignty—just the point about international law that I made above. Similarly, it would be nonsense to say that every political order must establish a rule of law for the ordinary situation. These are all contingent, historical formations. What we cannot have is the modern, Western nation-state without both. The nation-state has existed in the space of norm and exception. If this imagination of the political continues to be relevant to our situation, it is not because it expresses a timeless truth of politics. The point is much simpler: we, at least we in the United States, continue in the same long political tradition within which Schmitt found himself. Our imagination is informed by our deepest traditions of reason and will, of well-being and sacrifice, of the finite and the infinite.

CONCLUSION: EXISTENCE BEFORE ESSENCE

Insisting that we take up legal theory from the perspective of the exception is the fundamental point of disagreement between Schmitt and his jurisprudential interlocutors. This difference is the political side of a broader turn in European philosophy. "Existence precedes essence" is as good a motto for Schmitt's political philosophy as it is for Heidegger's philosophy of the individual. Like Heidegger's authentic individual, Schmitt's state always confronts the possibility of its own death. The sovereign is the political being characterized by this consciousness of the possibility of its own death. The state must first come into being; it must achieve it own existence. It must continue to will itself to be in the face of the acknowledgment of its own mortality. To flee from confronting the possibility of the death of the state is a kind of inauthenticity. To take up that knowledge is to achieve a kind of political authenticity.

The issue here is not to extol the virtues of the citizen soldier. Recognition of the historically contingent character of the state tells us nothing about whether its legal order should be supported, overthrown, or reformed. This recognition will, however, keep us from making empty claims about having reached the end of history. It may also cause us to reflect more deeply on the character of our own polity, which is most certainly committed to defending itself through invocation of the exception. In politics, as in individual life, the ordinary is first of all and most of the time a domain of inauthenticity.

When we today think that there are no exceptions because there is no longer any possibility of a threat to the existential character of the state, inauthenticity is exactly the right characterization of our attitude. We have no better sign of this inauthenticity than our approach to nuclear weapons, which make no appearance in the ordinary rule of law or in liberal political theory.[56] A political theory that does not account for this extraordinary threat is a poor theory. A legal practice that turns its gaze away fails to see the most obvious facts of our political life.

No nation has lived so close to the state of exception as we have since the birth of the nuclear age. Our position that we will threaten world destruction rather than surrender is exactly the meaning of capitulation today. Capitulation becomes a sovereign act of self-destruction that literally ends history in an expression of the infinite value of the nation. Nuclear weapons enact that convergence of destruction and construction that is the sovereign politics of exception and decision. The theory of the exception is just the direction in which we need to look if we are to understand what it was about the character of the political imaginary in the twentieth-century nation-state that made it possible for even a liberal constitutional order to find itself, in relatively short order, threatening to use—and even using—weapons of mass destruction. The end of history may come not with the arrival of the liberal democratic state but with what it is that state will do to defend its existence.

2

THE PROBLEM OF SOVEREIGNTY AS THE PROBLEM OF THE LEGAL FORM AND OF THE DECISION

POLITICAL THEOLOGY BEGINS WITH THE sovereign decision for existence. It places will before reason, the act before the norm. It understands the state from the point of view of the exception, not because it rejects the normal, but because the normal must be brought into existence and then sustained. At stake is not just a conflict of theoretical perspectives on the state but the character and locus of freedom. Only as a product of the will can we understand the state as an expression of freedom.

Having elaborated a theory of the sovereign decision in chapter 1, Schmitt moves on, in chapter 2, to a reconsideration of law—that is, the ordinary operation of legal norms—from the perspective of a political theological account of decision and will. In the course of this inquiry, it becomes clear that the earlier contrast of exception and norm was too simple: the decision is not just at the border of law but fully penetrates the legal order—and not just in the case of equity. It could not be otherwise, for politics is not a domain of freedom only in the exception but at every moment. If so, the judicial judgment must be reconceived.

Much of Schmitt's second chapter is taken up with a canvas of German legal theorists, who—apart from Kelsen—are not part of an American debate. The important point here is to understand what it was they were arguing about. For this purpose, it is enough to look at Schmitt's dispute with Kelsen, for this goes to one of the deepest issues of legal theory, then and now. That issue is suggested in the chapter's title, which juxtaposes the legal form to the decision. Just as the substitution of the specific idea of "popular sovereignty" for Schmitt's more general reference to sovereignty helped us in chapter 1, a substitution of "judgment" for decision can help in chapter 2: the problem is the judicial decision, that is, the judgment of a court. With this substitution, we are at the heart of a raging debate in American politics: what is the relationship between the appeal to legal form—for example, to the constitutional text—and the judgments of the Supreme Court? Schmitt argues that the form determines nothing. The decision—the act of will—is no less important here than in the exception.

If the relationship of form and legal decision were direct in the sense that text controls judgment, then we would not find ourselves battling so strongly over appointments to the Supreme Court. But if judgment does not follow form, is there any relationship at all between abstract norm and concrete decision? To ask that question is to move directly to the problem of interpretation. It has become a commonplace to observe that every judge needs a theory of interpretation. That theory fills the space between legal form and judgment: it is to explain the movement from an abstract text to an actual judgment.[1] In the United States, we never seem to reach closure on the question of which interpretive theory. Do we evaluate such a theory by its claim to democratic legitimacy, by its likelihood to produce just outcomes, by its fidelity to text, by its congruence with the professional ethos of lawyers, by its precedential support, or by some other standard? Displacing the argument over outcomes on to an argument over hermeneutics has not been a way to reach closure. Indeed, often we may more quickly and easily agree on an outcome than on interpretive theories.[2] Even were we to reach agreement on theory, the consequences for any particular decision would still be indeterminate, for a theory of interpretation can offer nothing more than yet another set of norms that themselves have to be applied to the concrete case.[3] We cannot avoid confronting the fact of the decision.

Schmitt's general point is perfectly accessible and quite compelling: we need to do legal theory from a perspective that recognizes the role of judgment. Law is not simply a system of formal norms. Mediating between form and judgment is not yet another theory but an act.

Schmitt's critique of Kelsen is that his theory of law never reaches the act of judgment. Kelsen, of course, recognizes that a norm must be interpreted before it is applied. He says that the norm can only supply a frame, which will often permit several different applications among which the decision maker must decide. But, for Kelsen, just when the moment of choice arises, the "pure theory of law" goes silent. About such discretion, legal theory has nothing to say. It is no longer interesting to the pure theory but to the sociology of law.[4]

Schmitt says of the decision that it is as if it "emanates from nothingness" (32). There will always be a gap between form and judgment. This is the same existential point that we saw in chapter 1: existence (the decision) precedes essence (the norm). We might offer sociological, psychological, or anthropological descriptions of the trend of decisions among a class or group, or even in the individual. To take this position seriously might lead us to the views of the American legal realist Jerome Frank, who thought that judges should set forth a kind of autobiography or psychological examination of themselves to explain their decisions.[5] Alternatively, we might think more seriously about the political legitimacy of the decision maker. Instead of legitimating the judgment by reference to a norm, we might refer to the representative status of the judge. In this direction, we might align ourselves with the nineteenth-century populists who mounted a political movement to have judges elected.[6] Finally, we might point to something unique about the judicial process as a method of dispute resolution, a process that works quite independently of the content of a particular norm.[7]

Schmitt does not move in the direction of either personal or political accountability in response to the problem of the running out of the legal norm. Nor is he interested in dissipating the significance of the moment of decision by focusing on the process by which it is reached. Instead, there is a short discussion of Hobbes who is "the classical representative of the decisionist type" (33). What interests Schmitt is Hobbes's insistence that power belongs to persons, not norms, and that power shows itself in a relationship of superiority of one person over another. Hobbes "rejected all attempts to substitute an abstractly valid order for a concrete sovereignty of the state" (33). Here, we find a connection between the decision that applies the legal norm and the decision for the exception discussed in the first chapter. Norms are constrained from above and below: they neither create nor apply themselves. They cannot preclude the exception, and they cannot sustain themselves. A state must will itself into being (there must be order brought out of chaos) but it must also will its continued existence (there must be judgments). A philosophy of law in the light of the sovereign function must be a philosophy of the will.

HANS KELSEN: LAW WITHOUT SOVEREIGNTY

Hans Kelsen, the dominant theorist of law in twentieth-century Europe, never had much of an impact or even appearance in the United States, despite the fact that he spent the last thirty-three years of his life working here. The obvious reason for Kelsen's failure here is that his jurisprudence of legal form has a focus that is quite the opposite of that of the legal realists who dominated the American scene.[8] Of the realists, one might say that they focused on the point of decision to the exclusion of form. Their interest was in applying the empirical social sciences—including sociology, psychology, and economics—to the problems of governance, whether through courts or administrative agencies. In part, this was a project of showing what judges actually do, an aspect captured in the idea of "prediction."[9] In part, this was a matter of applying the social sciences to the construction of law, that is, to what the law should be. For the realists, law in and of itself has no special claim in the formation of public policy. To think that law has a special claim or that there is a science of law that will of itself perfect the political order is to be the victim of false consciousness. It is to be captured by an ideology that makes one blind to facts. Their ambition was always to advance legal reform grounded in clear sight of the facts.

Generally, the legal realists thought of law as epiphenomenal: legal norms are the outcome of conflicts among organized interest groups. Norms are not something apart from politics but only local equilibria in the ongoing clash of interests.[10] The legal realists wholly rejected the approach of Christopher Langdell, the famous dean of Harvard Law

School, who claimed to find a science of law in the case-law method, an inductive science in which the cases support formal principles.[11] For the realists, it was not the concern with outcomes that was wrongheaded but the claim that the cases represent the working out of an abstract science of law that exists apart from—and prior to—the cases. A science of law could find a firm foundation in neither the legislature nor the courts, because questions of law were always questions of power.

Kelsen's pure science of law was hardly the same as Langdell's formal science of law. To the legal realists, however, the difference was that Langdell was wrong while Kelsen was irrelevant. Langdell was wrong because he thought there was a content to legal science; Kelsen was irrelevant because his idea of legal science was independent of any content. To understand Kelsen's problem in such a world, we can compare the realists' charge that claims to a special form of legal knowledge were "transcendental nonsense" to Kelsen's own appeal to a Kantian "transcendental" science of law. Felix Cohen characterized the transcendental nonsense of legal science as follows: "Legal science, as traditionally concerned, attempts to give an instantaneous snapshot of an existing and completed system of rights and duties. Within that system there are no temporal processes, no cause and no effect, no past and no future. A legal fixed decision is thus conceived as a logical deduction from fixed principles."[12] The Kelsenian pure science of law also knows no persons, parties, factions, or interest groups; it too excludes causes and effects.

Kelsen starts from Hume's simple and direct point that it is impossible to derive an ought from an is. Descriptive statements cannot ground normative claims. No matter how well we describe the mechanisms of coercion in a society, we cannot find in those descriptions any normative obligation. We can certainly derive objective predictions of the form, "If you don't do x, then you are likely to suffer consequences of the form y." But this does not tell me whether I should do x, only what may happen if I do not. Similarly, we can objectively describe the mechanisms for the production of legal norms. For example, the legislature is composed of representatives who decide through majority vote and follow *Robert's Rules of Order*. But whether the product they produce makes a normative claim is an entirely different matter. The mere fact of the legislature's existence is not sufficient to ground the normative weight of its laws. Calling a proposition "law" may tell me that the state is likely to use coercion to enforce compliance, but it is not enough to ground a claim that I ought to comply.

Consider an anthropological description of a foreign society, including its laws and mechanisms of enforcement. That description conveys no normative obligation for those who read it. An anthropological description of our own society will certainly capture the regularities of behavior that are involved in the production of law; it will also capture the regulatory effects that legal institutions may have on the society. But neither source nor effect, in themselves, will tell any person—whether or not he is a member—that he has an obligation to comply. The obligation simply cannot arise from a description: no ought can be derived from an is.

Arguments over the nature and source of legal obligation have been endless. If we accept the proposition that an is cannot create an ought, then we would seem to have two ways of constructing legal theory in response. We can approach law as a positive phenomenon with no necessary connection to an ought, or we can argue that it exists entirely on the normative side of the divide. The dominant form of Anglo-American jurisprudence chose the first option. For the legal positivists, there is no necessary connection between law and moral obligation. Some law, and some legal systems, may give weight to morally compelling norms, but that is a contingent social phenomenon, not something included in the very idea of law.[13] The compelling character of law must be found elsewhere: in the coercive command, in the usefulness of cooperation, in the advancement of personal ends, or in habits of compliance. The normative character of legal obligation as such is relative to context in the same way that the normative character of the rules of a game are relative. If I want to play the game, I must follow the rules. A social order should be thought of as a large, multiplayer game.

Of course, it is likely to be the case that most societies achieve some sort of relationship between the content of their law and their underlying moral beliefs. We have many reasons to want our legal obligations to coincide more or less well with our moral obligations. We don't want to be put to the choice; we don't want to be obliged to live a life we judge to be immoral. We may, accordingly, adopt some set of moral principles as legal side constraints—or supernorms—with respect to other laws. But even if this is a true statement with regard to the set of concerns we bring to the problem of the creation of law, it is not itself a condition of legality in general. Whether the law gets morality right is quite a different question from whether law is law. To deny this proposition is to take a natural law position, which holds that an immoral law is not a law at all. It cannot be because the immoral can generate no normative obligation.[14] On this view, it makes no sense to call something law, when it is properly viewed as a claim that should be resisted. In an age in which there is often substantial disagreement on the content of moral obligation, the position of natural law has not been widely attractive.[15] It is easier to describe a positive law as immoral than to describe it as not law at all.

Kelsen accepted completely the principle that no ought can be derived from an is. He also rejected natural law, placing himself entirely in the camp of legal positivism. Nevertheless, he thought that law is a system of normativity, that is, laws do convey an ought. If it is the case that no ought can be derived from an is, then the only source of a norm can be another norm. While law is normative all the way down, there is no reason to conflate the normativity of law with that of morality, the mistake of natural law. Law, Kelsen thought, is rather its own complete system of normativity, a kind of free-floating system of ought. One enters into or finds oneself a member of such a system of normativity in the same way in which one might enter into a system of religious belief. There can be multiple such systems of normativity, for example, law, religion, and morality.

One might think of the normative order of law as simply a disparate system of norms within which we find ourselves, rather like Wittgenstein's view of language. There would be no single proposition from which all others derived, although we could locate the source of each norm in another norm. Kelsen, however, was too much of a Kantian to think this way. Instead, he thought of the entire legal order as resting on a unique superior norm. All the single propositions of law in the system point back ultimately to this same ground, which he calls the "basic norm" or the "Grundnorm." Consider, for example, the way in which all legal obligations in the United States—at least federal legal obligations—point back to the Constitution as their normative ground. If not so grounded, the law is "invalid," meaning we have no legal obligation to comply.[16]

If norms can only derive from other norms, and if all legal norms are bound together in a unitary system, then there must be a single highest norm, a Grundnorm, from which the whole derived, a kind of foundational point that would be the font of all law. To accept that a proposition conveys a legal obligation means that one accepts the condition of normativity that infuses the entire system. Precisely because this Grundnorm is the point of origin to which everything refers as a necessary condition of normativity, it is a point that eludes speech within the system of norms that it makes possible. Indeed, we know we are at the Grundnorm when there is nothing further to be said. Here, the derivation of one proposition from another ends. We know that it must exist because this is a transcendental condition of the law that we do experience.

The Grundnorm is the point that provides the normativity of the Constitution, for example. What exactly are we to say about that, at least within the juristic form of speech? It must exist, but there can be no argument in support of its existence. If anything could be said, the possibility of questioning the ground of this norm would open up. If we could again ask that question, we would only push further toward the truly unspeakable Grundnorm. Kelsen liked to draw an analogy between the legal order and the religious order. At the Grundnorm, we are close to the traditional Jewish view of God as the creative source whose name cannot be spoken.

Kelsen's basic distinction of the ought from the is, of norms from facts, is reflected broadly in his division of legal scholarship into jurisprudence, on the one hand, and sociology, on the other. The former studies norms as norms; the latter studies the actual character and working of the state in the same manner that any other science might investigate objective phenomena. For the latter, a causal analysis is appropriate. We can ask what are the conditions—historical and material—under which certain kinds of behavior, including the generation of legal norms, take place. If, for example, a legal norm authorizes a majority of the legislature to make laws, we will still be interested in studying who the representatives are and what interests drive them. Those interests may explain the legislators' behavior even while they do not explain the normative consequences of that behavior.

For jurisprudence, on the other hand, there is no place for such causal analysis. One norm does not emerge from another as the effect of a cause. Their normative character is not caused at all. Of Kelsen, Schmitt writes: "To obtain in unadulterated purity a system of ascriptions to norms and a last uniform basic norm, all sociological elements have been left out of the juristic concept" (18). Schmitt immediately expresses his skepticism about this wholesale importation of the Humean distinction—one that might be true in moral theory—into the domain of law: "The application of disjunctions emanating from another discipline or from epistemology appears to be the fate of jurisprudence" (18). Must we choose between Kelsen's jurisprudence of norms or the legal realists' sociology of legal behavior? Neither approach leaves room for the free act.

Whatever criticism we might have of Kelsen, we can certainly understand the intuitive basis of his approach. If we inquire what is the source of a legal obligation—say a statutory rule—we can imagine two forms of response. A political scientist might describe the source in what Kelsen and Schmitt refer to as "sociological" terms. He might speak of voting blocks, of interest groups, of congressional strategy, of pork barrel politics, and of trading votes among representatives. He might place the statute in a broader political history, explaining how and why a particular regulatory regime has emerged as it has over a long period of time and to which interest groups it responds. He might go on to point out the interests at stake and who are the likely winners and losers. This information is relevant not just to the academy. The politician, in determining how to vote, may consider these same factors. But if that same norm comes before a judge, or is analyzed by a lawyer in the course of an argument before a court, the source of its quality as a "legal" obligation will look entirely different. We will no longer hear about interest groups, power, deals, or strategy. All of these "sociological" factors drop from view. Instead of a causal account, we will hear an account of derivation of one norm from another. To answer the question why this norm is a law, we refer only to higher-order legal norms.

The question before a court is whether a proposition is a valid norm, that is, whether it has the legal effect that it purports to have. To answer that question, the court must show that the possibility of this norm is already "contained" in a superior norm: did the superior norm authorize this norm? We might argue about how one demonstrates that possibility: this is the much-debated question of interpretation. At issue is how we decide that one norm derives from another. When the justices disagree about the constitutionality of a law, they are usually not disagreeing over what the legislature did or why it did it. Rather, they are disagreeing over whether this was a legislative possibility contained within the superior norms of the Constitution. This can be a startlingly difficult question to answer. But a theory of interpretation that crossed over into sociology would be a surprising move for a court. Indeed, it would be a category mistake. No court, for example, would call as witnesses the legislators who voted for the law—or the lobbyists who worked for its passage—to interrogate them about the normative content of the law. From the court's point of view, one law can only come from another law: it is derived, not caused. The legislators are, from this point of view, performing a legal—not a political—role. Their product is law not because of what they intended but by virtue of their complying with a normatively superior rule. This is what Kelsen has in mind when he excludes sociology from jurisprudence.

Moreover, while a court will pursue the hierarchy of legal norms in answering the question before it, that pursuit ends before the court reaches the Grundnorm itself. No court asks why it is bound by law at all. We do not find our Supreme Court wondering about the legal ground of authority of the Constitution itself. Were that question to come to the fore, the conditions would be open for a revolutionary act of reestablishing the legal order. We would, in other words, confront the Schmittian exception.

This double nature of inquiry into the law—normative derivation and empirical causes—is broadly analogous to Kant's theory of the relationship between morality and science, between freedom and necessity. Every actual event in the world is explained by setting forth its causes. Because it is caused, we cannot explain how the event could be otherwise, since every cause is itself caused. There is no place for normativity in a world of causal necessity because there is no freedom. Nothing can be other than it is. When we turn to human action, however, we are compelled to offer a parallel account that takes freedom as its first principle. This world is driven by norms and principles, not causes. Just as Kant believes that we give the moral rule to ourselves, Kelsen believes we give the Grundnorm to ourselves. To stay within the order of norms—one norm derives from another—is to stay within the domain of freedom.

We have no easy way of melding these two systems into one without reductionism in one form or another. Today, the reductionism tends to move in the direction of eliminating the normative: norms are explained biologically (pointing to such factors as evolutionary advantage or neurocircuitry) or they are explained sociologically (pointing to the influence of interest groups). Earlier, the reductionism ran in the other direction: physical phenomena were explained by pointing to God's plan or to the objective working out of reason. Contemporary reductionism produces the problem of meaning in a causally determined world; the earlier reductionism produced the problem of theodicy, that is, of evil in a world ordered by God. Most people are what we might call "everyday Kantians," believing that the two perspectives are simply parallel accounts of our human world. Context alone tells us to which account we turn: Are we asking a question about what we ought to do or are we explaining events in the world? Are we looking backward and explaining what happened or are we looking forward and deciding what we must do? Kelsen carries this duality directly into jurisprudence, making it a science of norms concerned with derivation, not causal explanation: "The basis for the validity of a norm can only be a norm; in juristic terms the state is therefore identical with its constitution, with the uniform basic norm" (19). The critical limit is "in juristic terms." Other terms will call forth other explanations.

Kelsen's insistence on unity and system means that there is no place for the sovereign command as the source of law. The fact that someone or some institution commands is only a fact, not a norm. It is, in effect, no different than the command of the robber with a gun: we might be well advised to comply, but we are not doing so out of a free act of forming our

will in congruence with a normative claim. We comply even while denying the normative character of the command. To use Hart's terms, we are
obliged but have no obligation.[17] Because the two comprehensive world-
views cannot come in contact, Schmitt accuses Kelsen of simply eliminating any place for a concept of the sovereign, if we mean by the sovereign a source of normative commands. Kelsen, in turn, accuses Schmitt
of reifying in the concept of the sovereign what is only a transcendental
condition of a legal judgment.[18] That which we label the sovereign can
only be a subject, natural or corporate, for it must be capable of decision. It is not another iteration of a norm but an actor in the world. As a
subject, it is on the wrong side of the fact/norm line to have any presence
within Kelsen's systematic unity of the law. "Kelsen solved the problem
of the concept of sovereignty by negating it. The result of his deduction
is that 'the concept of sovereignty must be radically repressed'" (21).

The legal order, on Kelsen's view, no more needs a sovereign source
than the physical order needs a sovereign source of miracles. In both cases,
nothing outside of the frame of explanation can enter into an account:
science does not have a place for God in its explanations of phenomena,
and law has no place for a sovereign command. God offers no explanation, when what it means to explain is to show how one event follows
another according to the laws of causation. Of God, Kant thought we
could say absolutely nothing because, in our world, to explain is to offer
a cause. Similarly, in Kelsen's jurisprudential world, to explain is to derive
one norm from another. There is no point at which the sovereign can
enter as a juridic subject in the explanation of what is and is not law. Both
sovereigns recede into the background. At best, they remain as matters
of faith about which nothing can or need be said. The physical world
is simply what is, carrying itself forward through laws of causality. The
normative world of the state is simply what makes a legal claim upon us,
carrying itself forward through principles of derivation.

NORM OR DECISION? THE IRREPRESSIBLE SOVEREIGN

Schmitt sees in Kelsen not just a misplaced philosophical intervention in
jurisprudence but a representative of a larger political misapprehension:

"This [the repression of the concept of sovereignty] is in fact the old liberal negation of the state vis-a-vis law and the disregard of the independent problem of the realization of law" (21). Liberalism prefers to focus on norms rather than power; in place of political conflict, it would rather argue about what the law is. The problem of the "realization of law," however, is never resolved at the level of the norm itself, for the norm is indeterminate over some range of outcomes. In law, we can't avoid the decision.

To decide is to decide both for and against. Those who lose are not necessarily, or even likely to be, enemies. But the possibility of political division is always there. Liberalism would deny the possibility of conflict by denying the place of the decision. Once we recognize that the decision resolves but does not end conflict, we see the connection of sovereign power to every decision. The legal resolution is only as strong as the promise to uphold the decision were conflict to erupt over it. We need not think that such a threat hangs explicitly over every decision, any more than we need to think that the state explicitly threatens to go to war with every potential enemy. In both cases, the sovereign threat informs the borders of the imagination. Doing so, it makes possible the ordinary situation.

Schmitt's critique of the tendency toward juridification of liberal politics anticipates the contemporary critique that liberals rely too heavily on the courts to achieve their political agenda, for example, with respect to issues of access to abortion or gay marriage.[19] This is not just a tactical preference for courts over politics. It rests on a denial of the possibility of opposition, or, more accurately, on an effort to close out the political space for an opposition. The reasoning is that if the courts say what the law is, and all are committed to the law, then the judgment of the court expresses that to which we are all already committed. Those who disagree are not understood as politically opposed but rather as mistaken in their understanding of the law. This desire to turn the opposition into the mistaken rests on the belief that the normative order of law is the order of reason itself: the completeness of law is the completeness of reason. Resistance is assimilated to irrationality. Believing that the political order should be the expression of reason, liberals have a tendency to believe that politics is or should be over. All that remains is for courts fully to articulate the content of the law.[20]

For Schmitt, law is not located on one side of a divide between the is and the ought. Rather, law exists at the intersection of the is and the ought. It contravenes this distinction imported from philosophy because there is no law outside of its application. We don't live in a world of abstract norms, any more than we live in a causally determined world. Rather, our experience is always that of facts already ordered by norms. This is true regardless of whether the norms are moral, religious, or legal. We live in a normatively ordered universe that we take to be the product of our own free acts. We find ourselves in this in-between state in which the abstract does not apply itself and the particular does not order itself. Neither exists without the other. Philosophy, including jurisprudence, goes wrong if it starts with either facts or norms; it finds it can never bring them back together. Both are abstractions from experience, which is always of meanings already operating in the world.[21]

Law is not a system of norms derived from one another but the realization of norms in the ordering of discrete situations. This point at which the ought becomes an is always eludes Kant, and Kelsen as well. It is exactly that which cannot be explained, if we start from the metaphysical distinction of is and ought. To develop legal theory from the standpoint of the decision requires shifting the focus from norms to sovereign, from essence to existence—or, from reason to will, for it is as willing subjects that we exist as free beings. The will discovers itself not as an abstract capacity but as already embedded in the objects of its creation. In Christian terms, it discovers that it has already sinned: there is no moment of human experience prior to the exercise of will.

Before we look in some detail at a jurisprudence of the will, we should be clear about the stakes. From Kelsen's point of view, the entire normative content of the state is a matter of law. A politics beyond law would be for him a politics of violence and coercion. It could not generate any normative obligation. There might, of course, be other normative systems—for example, religion—that intersect with political actions and demands, but legitimate politics is cabined by law. Accordingly, Schmitt complains of Kelsen's "negation" of the state. There is no place for the willed decision or for the personal responsibility that comes with the act of will. This is not far from how the judicial opinion represents the court's judgment: it offers a demonstration that the controverted act can—or cannot—be understood as the realization of a legal norm, which is itself embedded in an entire structure of norms arranged in a single hierarchy of authority. We have, however, no reason to take this self-representation as an accurate description of the act of deciding. Indeed, our contemporary disputes over the status and character of theories of interpretation stand as a challenge to this model of judicial decision making. The court would have us forget the act of judgment; it would have us forget that *it* is deciding. We should decline that invitation.

To grasp this question of the status of politics beyond law is to understand why so much of the contemporary argument about the concept of the exception focuses on what seems a merely formal issue: Is the exception, which is the suspension of the ordinary legal order, itself a lawfully regulated act?[22] Can law include the negation of itself in the decision for the exception or is that decision the moment at which the normative order of law gives way to a normative order of sovereignty? When the Israeli Supreme Court held that there could be no legal norm validating an act of torture but then added that a criminal defendant accused of torture may nevertheless have a necessity defense, it was demonstrating the paradoxes to which this question leads.[23] Torture is the exception outside of law, but the state may be legally justified in defending itself.

Exceptional moments of defense of the state against existential crisis were the focus of Schmitt's first chapter. His argument against Kelsen is not so dramatic, for Kelsen's view, he believes, does not even explain the ordinary character of a legal system. The problem of the decision is already present whenever a legal conclusion is supported by appeal to a superior norm. It arises just at the point when there must be a transition from an abstract norm to an actual ordering of events.[24] While Kelsen's pure theory of norms might be an adequate explanation of a rule-bound game like chess, in which the normative rules are quite independent of the decision about how to move, the pure theory does not capture the normative character of a political order. We do not argue about how a chess piece can move, but we are engaged in endless controversy about what actions can or cannot be taken as a matter of law. Law is not controversial just at the margins; rather, every legal claim is a subject of possible controversy. Put most simply, between legal norm and the facts, there must be a decision. We go wrong, however, if we think of norm and fact as two different domains that are each assessed independently, prior to the judgment. Norms and facts only emerge as such after the decision.

Decades later, Ronald Dworkin began his jurisprudential inquiry from the same insight. He moves, however, in exactly the opposite way from Schmitt. Dworkin puts all the weight on a theory of interpretation: legal controversy is interpretative controversy over what the law is.[25] He seeks resolution in an ascending frame of argument, appealing to broader and broader principles. Schmitt finds resolution in the opposite direction, that is, in the act of deciding. Both agree, however, that at stake in a jurisprudential theory is an account of law adequate to man's freedom. Their disagreement is as deep as can be: do we locate freedom in a norm or decision, in reason or will?

On Schmitt's view, we don't know what the law is until after the decision. The decision does not follow from the law, but the law follows from the decision. If this is so, then Kelsen is wrong at the most fundamental level: legal norms are not derived from other norms. Rather, they are the result of a decision that cannot itself be explained as a product of preexisting norms. It cannot be so explained because precisely what the law requires is controverted until the decision maker tells us the answer. This is a point that Robert Cover expressed sixty years later, when he observed that a legal order contains both a jurisgenerative and a jurispathic moment.[26] The former is law in the Kelsenian mode: norms endlessly proliferate from other norms. That process of proliferation gives us our disputes over theories of interpretation. Interpretation is a matter of bringing out the full range of meanings from a recognized norm—that range has no natural limits. Until and unless there is a practical conflict that requires resolution, there is no pressure for the jurispathic decision. We can talk until we are exhausted, only to return to the task of talking more after we rest.

This endless proliferation of derivations is the source of arguments about what we should hold the law to be. Legal interpretation is not limited to deductive forms of argument. It deploys analogy and meta-phor as well. It can, therefore, move in multiple directions at once. Legal argument can be as sprawling as literary interpretation. There are always a surfeit of analogies to draw. Such arguments about law are not, however, "the law." We cannot know which is the "right" analogy to draw until we know the decision. To the jurisgenerative moment, accordingly, must be added the "jurispathic" moment or, in Schmitt's terms, the moment of decision. The debate must be brought to an end by an act of decision. That decision will claim the authority of the legal form, but its author-ity does not derive from the norms themselves. It cannot because their meaning is endlessly debatable. Its authority is tangential to its legal form.

The normative order of law requires authority as much as that author-ity requires norms. Without authority, nothing happens; without norms, all that happens is arbitrary. While a court may want to collapse the one into the other as a matter of self-justifying rhetoric, the role of the theo-rist is to distinguish the jurisgenerative from the jurispathic. This idea is not entirely foreign to the judicial imagination and is well captured by Justice Jackson's famous and much-repeated quip that "we are not final because we are infallible, we are infallible because we are final."[27] The law is the product of the decision as much as of the norm. The court writes an opinion, but it also takes a vote. The opinion explains the norms, but that explanation may be no better (or even worse) than that of the dissent. What makes it the opinion of the court—and thus the law—is the vote.

If asked which has priority, norm or decision, we can only answer that this is the wrong question. We simply cannot have one without the other. Thinking in terms of norms and facts, however, will constantly mislead us into asking this question. We will, in that case, reproduce the conflict between Kelsen and the legal realists. Both sides try to understand legal order without taking account of the will. Schmitt, by putting exception and decision at the center of his thought, forces us to confront the will. The problem for theory—although not for an ongoing institution of legal practice—is to understand the intersection of reason and will in a way that is adequate to each. To articulate this middle path is the largest problem for legal theory today.

(This is Atria's project, see Adjudication and
the particular (2006)

Schmitt speaks to all of this quite directly in attacking those forms of jurisprudential thought that theorize law from a perspective that entirely eliminates the deciding subject, as if law were simply the endless articulation of reasons, one from another, to be applied to facts that exist independently of the norms. We need to give up the dichotomy and, instead, see the political world as the product of a free act. There are no facts apart from norms, and no norms apart from facts. The decision is the source of both.

The early-twentieth-century theorists who were the object of Schmitt's attack occupy a position somewhat similar to that of John Rawls today. Rawls believes that if we set the preliminary conditions of discourse in a rationally justified way—for example, behind the veil of ignorance— then the basic norms of a political order will emerge from the operation of reason itself. There is no place for the concreteness of an actual decision that is not itself derived from the formalism of the norms. Unanimity behind the veil is possible because will has been reduced to reason. Everyone would say exactly the same thing because, in the absence of different experiences, there would be no personhood.

The liberal effort to eliminate the personal from the law may have its historical origin in the political effort to free law from the king: "For Preuss and Krabbee all conceptions of personality were aftereffects of absolute monarchy" (30). We can do away with the monarch, but can we do away with the decision? Can we build a legal order that will be a "machine that would go of itself"? Schmitt thinks not: no decision, no law. "[A] decision in the broadest sense belongs to every legal perception" (30). A legal perception is not an abstraction, but an act of world construction. Schmitt offers his clearest statement of this point as follows: "Every legal thought brings a legal idea, which in its purity can never become reality, into another aggregate condition and adds an element that cannot be derived either from the content of the legal idea or from the content of a general positive legal norm that is to be applied" (30). That additional element is the moment of decision: the law is this, rather than that. Or more simply still, the view of one party rather than the other is the law. We see this visibly in an actual legal dispute, when both sides write briefs that may be equally plausible explanations of what the law means in the controverted context. If we think the role of the judge is to write an opinion that "explains"—that is, convinces—the losing party that his position was a "mistaken understanding of law," we are confusing law and pedagogy.[28]

The meaning of the law is simply indeterminate until there is a decision. If it were otherwise, the practice of dissent would not be possible— nor would the threat of reversal, which accompanies our practice of dissent. Were *Roe v. Wade* to be reversed, for example, the justification would not be that an exception has been made to the order of law. Rather, the opinion for the Court would take exactly the same form as a decision to affirm *Roe*: legal sources and methods of reasoning support this outcome, not the prior position. The "aggregate condition" would have changed by virtue of the decision. When we all agree, when there is no controversy, the issue may be decided, but it does not end up in court.[29] Conflict, even under law, highlights decision.

Contra Dworkin's argument, the judge does not decide between the parties' positions by referring to some third, or higher, norm within the law. To believe that possible is only an evasion of recognition of the willed act of decision. As Schmitt says, "every concrete juristic decision contains a moment of indifference from the perspective of content" (30). Both of the opposing briefs affirm the rule of law. The controversy arises precisely at the moment that the law as an order of norms is indifferent, meaning that we can tell two more-or-less equally compelling stories about the content of law. Controversial cases are not won because one side writes a brief that fails as a matter of law. The choice is never between law and nonlaw. The law will be affirmed whichever way the decision comes out.

The decision maker must decide. Deciding, he tells us what the law is: "The juristic deduction is not traceable in the last detail" (30). Only at the last detail, however, is the matter resolved one way rather than the other. This is just the point at which Schmitt disagrees with what Dworkin will later formulate as the "right answer thesis."[30] For Dworkin, the judge decides not by exercising his will but by locating a principle that determines the outcome. When faced with a choice between equally compelling principles, the judge is bound by that which better "fits" the aggregate of precedents. The specification of broad, overarching moral principles by the checking function of "fit" will be enough, according to Dworkin, to determine a concrete outcome. But to maintain this position, Dworkin has to refer to an imaginary judge, Hercules, who has perfect knowledge of principles and precedents.[31] Competition among conflicting narratives is resolved through Hercules's omniscience. For any actual judge, the process could only be "asymptotic," moving toward an ever-eluding, complete account. In the absence of that point of completion, however, a decision must be made. It must be made even when, as is usually the case, others are moving in a different direction along a different asymptote. It is only a matter of faith that all would converge at a "Herculean" point of perfect knowledge.

If we ask what the figure of Hercules—whose decision always represents the "true" meaning of the law—represents, we have no better answer than "the sovereign." He is that intersection of being and meaning, whose word is law. He stands in the Kantian tradition of freedom, which is found only in the giving of a rational rule to the self. The will is free, on this view, only when it is wholly rational. Hercules is a fiction that represents the democratization of sovereignty—each of us should aspire to be Hercules. That contemporary jurisprudence is still tied to such a figure should not surprise us: "The connection of actual power with the legally highest power is the fundamental problem of the concept of sovereignty. All the difficulties reside here" (18).

Schmitt captures the gap between norm and decision in striking language: "Looked at normatively, the decision emanates from nothingness" (31–32). The decision is not explained by the norm. Schmitt does not conclude from this that we must turn to sociology in order to explain the decision, although we might indeed be interested in sociological explanations of juristic behavior. This approach was enthusiastically adopted by many of the legal realists. Schmitt, however, is doing jurisprudence, not sociology. It is from a legal point of view that the decision comes as if from nowhere. It would be a mistake to think that the moment of decision represents the penetration of law by "causal and psychological" matters that do not belong in a legal system. The decision is not the corruption of law by nonlaw but a necessary element of a legal order. It is

the "determination of legal value" (30). Without the decision, law has
no more value than a work of fiction. "[T]he legal idea," he says, "cannot translate itself independently," by which he means it cannot judge a
"concrete fact situation" (31).

The decision is not an unfortunate consequence of our inability to
reason "all the way down." The decision is not the marginal space for
discretion left over from a failure adequately to specify a norm. Richer
norms will not eliminate the need for decision by reducing to the null
point the domain of discretion. Nor is the decision the lingering presence of an archaic personalism in the origins of law. It is, rather, a matter
of the character of a legal order; it cannot be otherwise. "Ascription is
not achieved with the aid of a norm; it happens the other way around. A
point of ascription first determines what a norm is and what normative
rightness is" (32). Existence before essence is true not just as a matter of
constitutional choice but at every moment in the life of the law.

Because law arises from decision, a critique of the decision which
argues that it misunderstood the norms does not bear on its legal
authority. Thus, Schmitt writes that a decision is "independent of the
correctness of its content." Or further, "The decision becomes instantly
independent of argumentative substantiation and receives an autonomous value" (31). Of course, whether we should comply with every legal
demand is another question. The point here is legal, not moral, authority. Neither lawyers nor citizens get to pick and choose which decisions
they want to afford legal recognition to; everyone, however, can choose
whether to comply. The legal scholar's role is to explain the entire body
of legal doctrine; he does not leave out some decisions as "wrong" but
rereads the whole to make sense of the parts. In Anglo-American juris-
dictions, this is reflected in the practice of teaching law through the case
method—at least as it is done today. No one today thinks that the cases
are the working out of the true science of the law. Rather, they are points
of ascription upon which the norms depend. The legal rule means nothing outside of the circumstances of its application. Paradoxically, we
might say that the reason it means little is that, in the abstract, it means
too much. We cannot know how it will order the future until we see how

it is applied. There must be a decision before we can understand what the norms require.

If we did not intuitively understand the importance of the decision for telling us what the law is, we would not invest so much political energy in our process of selecting judges. That energy is political, not legal. We don't give them a test on what the law is. We speak of "character"; we may speak of "judicial virtues" such as openness and respect. But the real drama, we know, lies beyond this. Even when we assume that every nominee will act, if appointed, in complete good faith, we know that between the norm and the decision stands a will that can only direct itself. What the subject brings to the decision is beyond words—it is "nothing"—from the juridical point of view. One does not write a brief, for example, appealing to the personal life histories of the judges, any more than one appeals to their personal politics. How we coordinate the interaction of these two points of view—of the political and the juristic perception—might be a fruitful subject for anthropological investigation.[32] The problem is not different from that of how we coordinate religious belief and a scientific outlook. We cannot find the answer in a theory of religion or of science. We must look to see how we actually live with incommensurable symbolic orders.

One objection to this analysis is to point out that law often specifies the formal position of the decider, although not the occupant of the office. We know the court decides; we don't know who will be on the court. The role of the judge is established, organized, and constrained by law. Law, as a system of norms, may be silent at the moment of the decision, but it is hardly silent about the location of the decider. Schmitt seems to say the contrary: "That the legal idea cannot translate itself independently is evident from the fact that it says nothing about who should apply it. . . . A distinctive determination of which individual person or which concrete body can assume such an authority cannot be derived from the mere legal quality of a maxim" (31). So accustomed have Americans grown to courts claiming the power "to say what the law is" that we might simply reject this proposition. In fact, it points to a very familiar characteristic of the American experience of law.

Perhaps the single most controversial proposition in American constitutional law has been the Supreme Court's claim in *Marbury v. Madison* that it is has the final authority to say what the law is. The argument against *Marbury* has been that "the legal idea [the Constitution] says nothing about who should apply it." There have been endless arguments that Chief Justice Marshall's claim for judicial supremacy was an unsupported claim, mere dicta, inconsistent with the departmental character of authority, a bold assertion of power, or wildly beyond the power of the Court to make good on for at least one hundred years. Schmitt's point inheres in this controversy: no norm can establish the authority of its own application. European states had constitutions with abstract legal norms, including the specification of individual rights, long before they located authority in a court to apply those norms in the evaluation of the constitutionality of other laws.

Every governmental actor will claim the power to decide what the law means insofar as a legal norm appears relevant to carrying out his or her responsibilities. Those determinations will be controverted. Judicial determinations are no less capable of being challenged by others than are executive determinations.[33] Americans have seen these controversies arise numerous times, starting as early as the Virginia and Kentucky Resolutions and then Jefferson's decision to pardon all those convicted under the Alien and Sedition Acts.[34] That we settle into habits of governance should not lead us to believe that the point of decision is either incontrovertible or settled once and for all. The disputes between Congress, the president, and the courts over the legality of elements of the war on terror remind us of the timeliness of Schmitt's claim that the decision comes to norm "as if from nowhere," but still it comes. We cannot answer the question of who decides by looking at the norms themselves.

More than that, we can see the close relationship between the claim to decide and the location of sovereign power. This was clear on its face in the early federalism disputes in this country, an example of Schmitt's assertion that the fundamental problem of sovereignty is the connection of "actual power with the legally highest power." Assertions of law without actual power are no more sovereign than are assertions of power without reference to law. Unable simply to write power into being along with the constitutional text, the framers spoke of "dual sovereignty." The lingering claim of sovereign authority of the states powered the major constitutional controversies in the nation right through the Civil War.

Sovereign authority is not the authority just to express a view on the application of a legal norm; it is the authority to make good on that view. There is, in the end, no distinction to be made between the authority to decide and the authority to conscript, that is, to use the violence of the state to put in place the decision. This is not to reduce the decision to coercion, but it is to suggest the stakes of a decision that says what the law is. Politics is not literary criticism. We are not debating the meaning of a text; we are asserting the authority of the state to bring one meaning rather than another into the world. Multiple claims of sovereign authority can lead to violent confrontation since there is no norm to which one can appeal to settle disputes. That violence does not break out has nothing to do with the norms but with the habits, beliefs, and expectations of a population. We may disagree on the meaning of the norm, yet we may simply not care all that much about the decision, or we may converge in our expectation of who is to decide, or we may be attached to each other on other grounds that make violence unimaginable. Among friends much can be disputed; among enemies, any dispute can lead to violence.

Despite the recurrent theoretical problem of the counter-majoritarian difficulty, Americans now take it more or less for granted that the Supreme Court has the final power to decide, to tell us what the law is. The questions of how that belief came to be and how it is sustained are not merely of historical interest. Rather, we want to know how the Court presents itself to the community's political/legal imagination in exercising the power to decide. What we find is that the Court's decisional authority is inseparable from its claim to speak in the voice of the sovereign people. This is exactly the way in which the Court asserted its authority in *Marbury*: the voice of the Court is the voice of the People.[35] Its voice transcends that of a politically representative institution, and it is certainly not that of a collection of individuals who are each expressing their best interpretations of the text. The high rhetoric of the Court tracks the fundamental structure of the American political imagination: the sovereign people produced the constitutional text. Reading that text to us, the Court recovers that sovereign voice. This is not the moral authority

of Hercules but the political authority of We the People. This is a rhetorical assertion that the Court must always work as a political body to
maintain.[36] When it fails in that task—as it did, for example, in *Dred Scott*
and in its confrontation with Roosevelt over the New Deal legislation—
its claim to be the best interpreter of the text will be challenged by those
who make an alternative claim to sovereign authority. Elected officials
will claim a power to decide and the issue will be whether they can make
their view of the law real.

If we think that we can locate the power to decide by studying the
place of the sovereign in the constitutional scheme, we are mistaking
logic for experience. Power is never a matter of theory but of existence.
The equation works in the opposite direction: wherever we find the
assertion of the power to decide what the law is, we will find an assertion of sovereign presence. For example, with respect to foreign policy
and national security, the Court has traditionally been at its weakest
point in asserting an identity with We the People, while the president
has been at his strongest. The issue is not one of better "representing"
the national interest. Rather, we have seen the nation through the president in moments of national crisis: his rhetorical role is to present the
nation to itself, configuring himself as the universal, sacrificial citizen. If
he is successful—and arguably he is becoming less likely to succeed—the
power to decide shifts to him. Fully to understand this, we must turn
from the theology of creation to that of Christology as the frame of the
imagination, for the question is no longer one of miraculous creation
but of who embodies the whole. Here, it is enough to say that a system
of norms cannot, of itself, order a concrete factual situation. The passage from the abstract to the concrete, from potential to actual, from
fiction to history requires the decision. The legitimacy of the decision
cannot come from the norms, but neither can it undermine the norms.
It is bound to the norm but outside the norms.

CONCLUSION

Two generations later, Dworkin is writing in response not to Schmitt
but to the double challenge of the legal realists and the legal positivists.

Against both, he wants to assert the role of moral reasoning within the law. Contra the realists, law is not an epiphenomenon to be explained by the empirical social sciences. It is not a function of judicial psychology, of class interests, or of economic determinism. The judicial decision is to be explained from within the discipline of law as the consequence of principles with moral weight, not as a function of causal forces—whether of individuals or of groups—outside of law. Contra the positivists, Dworkin argues that there is no point at which the resources of law drop aside and we are left with only a "political" decision. Hart had argued that a legal norm has a core and a periphery.[37] Within the core, we could talk about application of the rule. But once outside of that core, to say that the decision maker is applying the law veils the reality of judicial "discretion," a political act. Dworkin argues that there simply is no place at which the norms give out. We resolve interpretive debate not by going outside of law but by reaching further into the normative resources. Law is an effort to shape political reality under a principled vision. Its end is the construction of a state of political affairs—as well as private relations—that express our understanding of how these relations ought to be structured. Law just is the effort to create a moral life together.

Dworkin's ideal judge—Hercules—carries on the enterprise of principled interpretation of the existing legal materials as long and as far as necessary to reach a decision. Since there is a "right answer," which is principled all the way down, the aspiration of law is to be a system of reason. At no point do we confront the brute fact of power, of the decision that cannot explain itself. Whenever law speaks, it speaks with integrity, meaning it speaks in the voice that every person would use were he or she able to think the matter through thoroughly. Hercules is an idealized version of judge, scholar, citizen—all of whom blend into each other in the empire of moral reason that is law.

Counterposed to Dworkin's view of the empire of reason is Foucault's understanding of the microdynamics of power. Foucault too is skeptical of the place of the decision as a free act. For Dworkin, no decision is needed because Hercules will always find the resolution outside of himself in a principle. Hercules has no will as a subject, which is exactly why he can be an ideal character. On Foucault's analysis, decision is not

possible because power—not principle—overflows the frame of decision. In *Discipline and Punish*, for example, he writes:

> The general juridical form that guaranteed a system of rights that
> were egalitarian in principle was supported by these tiny, everyday,
> physical mechanisms, by all those systems of micro-power that are
> essentially non-egalitarian and asymmetrical that we call the dis-
> ciplines. . . . The real, corporal disciplines constituted the founda-
> tion of the formal, juridical liberties.[38]

Power works in a continuous, microdynamic framing of every possible
proposition, that is, every imaginable outcome.

For Foucault, no one can reach a Herculean perspective because outcomes are determined well before the principle in its abstract character
is apprehended. Power is at work in the imaging of the project and in the
imagination of the self in relationship to that project. Dworkin offers a
kind of ideal self-reflection of the judge: attempting the Herculean task
is how the judge imagines himself. It is not surprising that the judge in a
liberal society understands himself as acting under a moral principle. It
is surprising, according to Foucault, that theory would bind itself to this
self-conception of the judge. Theory's role is not be an adjunct to power;
rather, it should itself be a space of freedom.[39]

The theory I have sketched in this chapter occupies a position
between the theories of Dworkin and of Foucault. Like Dworkin, I
reject the distinction between the core and the periphery, which grounds
the distinction between law and discretion for the legal positivists. But
while Dworkin argues that discretion never begins, I argue that there
is no core. No legal norm, no matter how clear we might think it to be,
applies itself. There is a gap between norm and application always and
everywhere. That we might not be aware of it in "easy cases" just tells us
that there is unanimity at this moment on the nature of the decision. It
does not tell us that the norm is driving the unanimity. On this point,
I am closer to Foucault: unanimity points to power, not to an essential
truth. Thus, most Americans were fully capable of maintaining slavery
while believing in the moral norm of equality. That we can no longer

do so does not mean that the norm is now determining the facts, only that we have reached a particularly stable point from which we imagine instances of equality.

If we shift from slavery to affirmative action, we find that we get very little guidance from the norm of equality. Dworkin would tell us that we only need to engage seriously with the principle of equality as it has played itself out in American legal history to resolve the controversy.[40] About that, we are entitled to be skeptical. The contrasting views on the question don't seem to be any less principled. Nor are we at the periphery, as opposed to the core. We simply have a deep disagreement about how the principle of equality orders this factual situation. We have no reason to think that talking the matter through will bring us to agreement. Not because one side is principled and one side is not, but because only after the issue has been decided will we know what the legal principle of equality means. The meaning of the norm follows from the point of ascription, not vice versa.

Against Foucault's position, I argue for the need for a decision. Power remains an attribute of subjects. There is a who—a subject—that decides. The decision is not dissipated in the complexity of organizational life or the structured character of perception. Something must be done; an act must be taken. The principle does not apply itself without a judicial decision. Whether that decision will settle the matter or only lead to further disagreement—and what will be the consequences of that disagreement—depends in large part on whether we are friends or whether we might become enemies.

With power comes personal responsibility: the sovereign acts and is held accountable. That accountability may look like revolution in the streets. Sometimes the sovereign loses his head; sometimes he is simply ignored; sometimes he is defeated by other claims to speak in the sovereign voice. Judges, because they decide, face the same spectrum of accountability: they can be attacked, impeached, displaced, or ignored. The exercise of power is never harmless for the actor or the victim. The political remains a domain in which individuals matter because the decision is theirs to make. Neither reason nor power alone will do the work of the political.

The decision is the free, creative act. It is, therefore, the moment of responsibility. For Dworkin, there is no such moment of responsibility. Ideally, Hercules makes no decision at all. Hercules speaks what everyman would say were he able to speak from a position of pure practical reason. Foucault too dismisses the moment of decision. Notwithstanding his rejection of anything like Hercules, he has the same urge to dissipate the decision in the discourse of everyman: not what everyman would say, but what all are saying. We see here the double form of the dissipation of the sovereign voice characteristic of contemporary thought. In one direction, the sovereign becomes only an abstract ideal; in the other, it is decentralized into the mass of ordinary citizens all speaking the same thing. Whatever free speech might mean to Hercules, Foucault reminds us that someone actually speaking a free—that is, an original—thought may be among the hardest things in the world to find.

One of the striking features of our actual legal system is the manner in which our courts become multimember bodies as we advance up the judicial hierarchy. They reach a decision with a vote. The vote decides what the law is, even though the statement of the law—the opinion—will never directly attribute the law to the vote. Similarly, no such vote can appear in Dworkin's theory: Hercules always decides the case by himself. For Foucault too, the vote is irrelevant because he has no way of theorizing the significance of disagreement within the court. Schmitt understands the critical role of the vote: it is the decision.

Judges try to explain the decision in an opinion. We are free to think that the dissent makes a better argument. We are not free, however, to believe that the law is as the dissent describes. Decision determines norm. A theory of law must, accordingly, theorize the moment of decision, not as something that comes from outside of law—the mistake of the legal realists—but as something that comes from outside of the norms. The rule of law is as much about decision as it is about norms. It cannot be about one without the other. When we take up the problem of the decision, we are led back to the issue of sovereignty. The rule of law is the will of the sovereign, not because the sovereign has some ideal knowledge, but because the decision is the locus of sovereign presence. That presence, it should be becoming clear, is the locus of freedom within the conditions of the political.

3

POLITICAL THEOLOGY

LIKE THAT OF THE FIRST CHAPTER, the opening line of this chapter has entered the canon of political theory: "All significant concepts of the modern theory of the state are secularized theological concepts not only because of their historical development—in which they were transferred from theology to the theory of the state, whereby, for example, the omnipotent God became the omnipotent lawgiver—but also because of their systematic structure, the recognition of which is necessary for a sociological consideration of these concepts" (36). Here, we are at the very heart of the matter: What exactly is political theology? How does it differ from other forms of jurisprudence and political theory? Why is it an important supplement to those other forms of inquiry?

Schmitt hardly offers direct answers to these questions. Nevertheless, two points emerge as essential in this chapter. First, political theology explores the relationship between a basic model of political order—a conception of the character and sources of legitimacy—and a contemporaneous theological model. Schmitt argues that every era has a common way of thinking about order, which connects the political and the metaphysical.[1] Second, political theology deploys a methodology that he calls "a sociology of concepts." That methodology, I will argue, remains central to the political theological enterprise, even as the modern political imagination has broken decisively with the metaphysics of our era. The conditions of postmodern inquiry have become so diverse as to overwhelm

Schmitt's substantive claims. That diversity could itself become a principle of unity—in both theory and politics—is not an idea that Schmitt could imagine. Despite this, his methodology, which looks to both the historical development and systematic structure of concepts, remains the compelling way of exploring what I referred to above as the "historical a priori" or the "social imaginary."

Schmitt contrasts a sociology of legal concepts with an ordinary sociological approach to law. At issue in this contrast is the place of causality in the production of concepts. Sociology is an empirical science, meaning that its explanations rely on a principle of causality. A sociology of law seeks to explain the relationship of legal concepts and institutions to other social formations. The relationship is assumed to be causal. Sociologists do argue about the direction of the causal chain. Some believe that the content of the law is caused by the material interests of individuals and groups; others argue that the causal direction runs from ideas—including law—to material distribution. At issue are different understandings of the sources of power—material or ideological. The form of causal explanation, however, is shared. The sociology of concepts, on the other hand, rejects the principle of causality as the form of explanation. Once again, a concept of freedom is at stake, for no free act—including a free thought—can be understood as the consequence of a cause. This chapter, accordingly, is continuous with the last two in its underlying concern with freedom. But now, the freedom of theory—the freedom of the philosopher—is at stake.

SOCIOLOGY OR THE SOCIOLOGY OF CONCEPTS?

If earlier Schmitt took Kelsen as his antagonist, here his target could be thought of as Max Weber. The traditional sociological approach to law investigates the relationship between forms of legal understandings and the interests and practices of particular groups of individuals. Weber, for example, sees a relationship between the rational structure of modern law and the life practices of bureaucrats. Bureaucratic organizational structure replicates itself in the nature of legal thought—think, for example, of a "decision tree"—just as modern legal thought expresses itself in material form in bureaucratic organization.

It is no more than common sense to think that social practices and ideas are in a reciprocal relationship. My beliefs must make it possible to carry out the functions that define my role; they must make sense of my place in the world. If they do not—if ideas and practices are discordant—there must be some external factor that maintains the stability of role. I can be coerced into mechanically performing tasks that I fail to understand or that I think are wrong. Coercion can take the hard form of threat or the soft form of incentive. If the former, my self-understanding will likely refer not to the role but to my sense of myself as victim: not craftsman, but slave. If the latter, my self-understanding will distinguish between my apparent role and my "true" function: not craftsman, but supporter of my family. Generally, roles and beliefs come to match each other over time. Coercion requires too many social resources to sustain indefinitely, while cognitive dissonance requires too many psychic resources. Of course, one can fill more than one role at a time, and there is much variation—individual and social—in how much dissonance can be suppressed or overcome.

It is difficult, for example, to be a bureaucrat in the modern welfare state without thinking first that there is a privileged place in law for expert knowledge, and second that there is a relationship between the application of that knowledge and the public good. The enthusiasm of the bureaucrat for the ideals that express the epistemic and normative character of his role is a familiar phenomenon both in fiction and fact. If, instead, I think that relationships of law are to reflect the weight of familial relationships or to build on the subjective preferences and personal ties of those with governmental authority, I am a bureaucrat in form only. Bureaucracy requires an entire culture. Where that culture is lacking, efforts to create a bureaucratic role usually fall to one form of pathology or another.

To imagine a bureaucratic role is already to imagine an entire conceptual order that includes ideas about the sources of legitimacy of law, as well as about the possibility of realizing the truth of those beliefs. If

I did not think that people could act as required by the abstract specification of a norm, then I would not imagine a legal order that required bureaucratic administration. If I did not think that it was legitimate for government agents to ignore personal relationships in the application of general rules, then I would have no way to understand why a modern government should be organized as a bureaucracy. Assigned a bureaucratic role, I would simply not understand what it was that I was to do. More precisely, I would understand instead that I am to use the public power given to me for personal, familial, or group ends. The same, of course, can be said about the role of judging or policing: without an imaginative structure in which the function is embedded in forms of knowing and norms of being with others, the person called a judge or law officer will be serving purposes other than those we associate with the role. Imagination and function are bound together not because all roles are embedded in the logic of means-ends rationality, but because only as self-directed agents can we rely upon each other; only then can there be a self-reproducing stability in the social order. We direct ourselves according to our ideas of who we are and what it is that we can and should do. If we fail, we judge ourselves to have acted wrongly. That is what it means to be a moral agent. The point of arguing in the last chapter that norms are indeterminate without a decision was not to deny moral responsibility for sustaining norms. Just the opposite: it was to focus on the responsibility to create and sustain the norm in the decision.

Bureaucratic functions, then, are as much a product of administrative rationality as they are the cause. One cannot imagine the role absent the possibility of the ideas; one cannot imagine having the ideas absent the possibility of the role. If conceptual order and function are reciprocal, then there is no single direction of causality. We have no reason to think—in fact, we have every reason not to think—that an imaginative structure emerges prior to the social functions that put the concepts to use. That would be like thinking that a language emerges prior to people actually speaking or religious beliefs emerge prior to a practice of faith. With respect to social meanings, ideas shape practice, while practice shapes ideas.

Schmitt's basic argument with sociological accounts is not over the direction of causality but over the adequacy of a causal account in either direction. Nevertheless, even within sociology, he thinks it a mistake to try to reduce the relationship of ideas and practices to one that moves in a single direction only. Theoretical unity is accomplished at the cost of what Schmitt describes as "caricature" or what we would call reductionism (43). He offers examples of such reciprocally reductionist approaches. To think that material function produces ideology is the approach of Marx: ideology, for the Marxist, is always a function of the economic order. A modern example of material reductionism is the effort to explain ethical beliefs on evolutionary grounds.[2] To think that ideas produce material functions is the Hegelian approach of thinking that the political order just is the working out of objective Reason. A modern example of reductionism in the direction of ideas is Fukuyama's theory of the end of history.[3]

Both forms of reductionism continue to dominate much of legal theory.[4] There is no shortage of those who think that political beliefs, including beliefs about law, are a product of material interests—for example, the earlier legal realists and many who today pursue positive political science. Their mantra might be "trace the money." For them, ideas are always epiphenomenal. Similarly, there are those who believe that practices are simply the expression of ideologies—for example, feminists who trace inequality in law to patriarchal ideologies or those who think that free-market capitalism is a function of a libertarian ideology. A background belief of many today is that we can explain the history of Western politics as the working out of liberal ideas about the nature of individual dignity. The practice of an international law of human rights is put forth as the realization of these ideas. That belief is often matched by an opposing idea that Western political ideology is a function of the pursuit of material interests. In considering foreign policy, we are often unsure whether democratic ideals are a consequence or a condition of market capitalism. The result is we don't know how "to manage" a transition.[5] Management, of course, assumes there are causal relationships to be directed.

In political thought and practice, we pursue both forms of sociological speculation all the time. We think of the ways in which the interests of different groups are reflected in their understanding of the legal order.

Businessmen are likely to think that at the core of the rule of law is the protection of property and contract. Religious groups will think that the constitutional protection of the private has more to do with protecting conscience and church than with protecting property and contract. Legal interpretation emerging from the legislative branch is likely to emphasize checks on presidential power, while that from the executive is likely to emphasize the broad discretionary power of the commander in chief. At the same time, we are interested in instances in which individuals and social groups act counter to these factors of material self-interest. Then, we say, they acted on principle, as if behavior isn't always expressing one principle or another.[6] We want our politicians to advance our interests and to stand on principle, just as we want this of ourselves. While we live with this tension, sociology is always in danger of resolving it in one direction or the other.

A sociological point of view, of course, need not become a form of determinism. Each person certainly has the capacity to critically analyze his practices and beliefs, even if first of all and most of the time that capacity is not exercised. It may be psychologically difficult, but it is possible to give up a career and become a Buddhist monk, just as it is possible to reshape one's ideology. We understand our limits and those of others, but we don't think these limits are given from outside of ourselves such that we are not properly held accountable for them.

Nor need we think that any of the ordinary connections of ideas to practices are made in bad faith. The point is just the opposite: we expect belief and social role to meet in the imagination. Beliefs must make possible the life I lead, just as that life gives the force and direction to certain ideas over others. When we ask how class, family, career, or group identity shape political beliefs, we are pursuing the subjects of classic sociology. When we ask how ideology shapes self-identity and group formation—whether of ethnicity, gender, or class—we are pursuing the subjects of contemporary sociology. Structurally, the project is the same, although the direction of inquiry may be different.

In neither classic nor contemporary sociological inquiry, however, are we pursuing what Schmitt calls the "sociology of concepts." About all such "partial" accounts, Schmitt says, "both the spiritualist explanation of material process and the materialist explanation of spiritual phenomena seek causal relations. At first they construct a contrast between two spheres, and then they dissolve this contrast into nothing by reducing one to the other" (43). Thus, of Max Weber, Schmitt writes, "he traced the differentiation of the various legal fields to the development of trained jurists, civil servants who administer justice, or legal dignitaries" (44). To look for causation in this direction—from roles to ideas—fails to rise to the level of the concept: "it involves the determination of a certain kind of motivation of human action" (44).

Schmitt is not dismissing sociology; he is not denying that social and psychological inquiry have any relevance or offer any insight. When he describes such reductionist approaches as "psychological," or says that they are the sorts of approaches that one finds in "brilliant literary criticism" (45), we should see an affirmation of the importance of these forms of inquiry. We cannot do without psychology in either its individual or social forms. There is nothing wrong with literary criticism. We do need to think about the material motivations of ideas if we want to act toward others without prejudice or bias and if we want to understand where others are coming from. We also need to think about our own ideological predilections. We cannot deny that there are such causal relationships in both directions. We do, however, need to avoid what Schmitt calls "caricature," which arises precisely when we think that we are intellectual prisoners of such causal factors, whether material or ideological. We would remain in the domain of caricature, even if we were to combine both approaches to causal relationships, recognizing the reciprocal relationship of the material and the conceptual.

The real problem is in the idea of causality between two separate spheres, not in the direction of the causal forces. Causal accounts are the form of sociological explanation. The rejection of causality has first to be understood in light of the work of the first two chapters, which insisted that a political order can never be accounted for through the operation of norms alone. The decision is the free act. Exception and judgment are expressions of a free will. That will, I argued, acts in response to the norm without being determined by the norm. A sociological explanation would fill the space between system and exception, or norm and judgment, by a causal account. Doing so, it would deny the possibility of politics as a domain of freedom. We have made no progress at all in our understanding of the free will if we escape from determination by norms only to be captured by determination by causes.

A sociology of concepts must be understood as a practice of free thought. Schmitt is, accordingly, particularly concerned with the way in which the ordinary sociological approach necessarily reflects back on the work of the scholar himself. Here too, ideas can be reduced to a function of role. Taking this perspective, we end up saying things like, "the Hegelian system . . . would have to be characterized as the philosophy of the professional lecturer . . . or it would be possible to view Kelsen's jurisprudence as the ideology of the lawyer-bureaucrat practicing in changing circumstances, who . . . seeks to order systematically the positive decrees and regulations that are handed down to him" (44–45). We lose any possibility of imagining or recognizing free thought. Indeed, the very aspiration for such freedom of thought becomes just another belief to be accounted for by material circumstances.

Schmitt, it turned out, was right to express this worry, for, as much as any twentieth-century thinker, he has suffered this fate. Scholars try to explain the link between his own political circumstances and the content of his theory. Again, we see the double direction of causal reductionism in such sociological accounts. Some argue that Schmitt was attracted to National Socialism because of his theory of the political, while others argue that his theory reflects the political and material crises of Weimar.[7] In neither case do we respect his thought. To import causality into the domain of thought makes such respect impossible. When Schmitt insists on a "sociology of concepts," rather than a sociological approach, he is not just insisting on the integrity of ideas, he is defending the very possibility of philosophy as a practice of freedom.

At stake as well is how we should frame our material expectations of philosophy. Just as we must not reduce ideas to material context, we should not give too much weight to the claim that our ideas will have a direct effect upon the world. This is an important cautionary statement about the practical possibilities of philosophy. Political practices are not particularly responsive to theory. It is not that the practices are inert or determined by material causes; rather, they are never mere applications. They are expressions of an entire world of meaning. To change a political practice may require that we change an entire world.[8] We cannot look for an explanation of the rise of National Socialism in the philosophy of Nietzsche. The practice of Soviet politics cannot be attributed to the thought of Marx. Politics is not a matter of realizing the truth of an idea, and getting your theory right may have little to do with practical politics. Liberal political theorists constantly indulge this presumption of thinking that the demonstration of the fundamental principles of liberalism will lead to progressive reform of the liberal state. They are constantly dismayed by the failure of practice to follow theory. But it is only a presumption of the theorist to believe that practice is the application of theory. This is, in Schmitt's term, "caricature."

The point, then, is not to discover a causal relationship running in both directions but to break with the idea of causality. We should not think of practice and idea as causally interacting across a kind of ontological divide, as if the practice is a "thing" in the world and the idea a subjective phenomenon. Practice is never just an application of a norm; it is a way of communicating. Practices only become possible within a community that "knows" what they mean. The relationship of practice and idea is better understood on the model of discourse—each side is communicating meanings. A legal decision is a practice in just this sense: it is not the mechanical application of an abstract rule but a judgment— that is, a statement—of what the law is.[9] This reciprocal, discursive relationship is true not just of the particular judgment but of entire roles, including that of the judge or lawyer. Living under the rule of law is not a technique of means-end rationality, as if one uses legal forms only to reach exogenous ends. Rather, the rule of law constitutes a way of living; it links subjects and practices in a single world of meaning.[10]

A practice should not be thought of as merely the outcome of a course of reasoning; it is not like the discovery of an object based upon a prediction. It is not the end of discourse but is itself a form of discourse. A practice always expresses a symbolic content; it stands to ideas in the same way that a proposition does. We communicate with each other and with ourselves through social practices as much as through language. I know what it means to encounter a bureaucrat; I know this before either of us speaks a word. The social imaginary, which holds ideas and practices in a reciprocal unity, is not something "in our heads" but in the world, in the same way that language is in the world. If we ask how it got there, we must turn to genealogy; if we ask how it maintains itself, we must turn to a study of its "systematic structure."[11] Living in a world of meanings in every direction, we live freely.

None of this means that practices and ideas are perfectly in sync. We press our ideas in the service of our practices, but we reform our practices as we reflect upon our ideas. In the tensions between the two, we often find that which we argue about. This is often the method of common-law adjudication, for example. Because practices carry meanings, we should not think that practices and ideas are actually opposed to each other as separate spheres: both are symbolic structures set in an internal discourse, speaking a single language—or at least dialects of the same language. To be a self-conscious agent is to question oneself, and those questions move simultaneously in both directions: What do I think? What must I do? Linking both is the third great Kantian question: in what must I have faith?[12] There may be no better example of these relationships than adjudication. These are questions of thought, action, and faith that the judge poses to himself. He answers when he writes an opinion to explain his decision. We deny the meaning of that act when we "explain" it either by locating the judge in a particular interest group or by seeing the result as only the application of a norm.

We can think of the relationships of ideas and practices here on the model of Thomas Kuhn's theory of the relationship between paradigms and revolutions in scientific thought.[13] Most of the time, changes in ideas and practices occur in the mode of "ordinary science," with modest innovations on each side pushing reforms in the other. The judge asks what the implications of a precedent are. He treats it as a paradigm and asks what it means for his present case. As I explained in the last chapter, however, it is just as accurate to say that in deciding the case, the judge determines what the meaning of the precedent is. Deciding *Casey*, for example, the Court tells us the meaning of *Roe*, even though the opinion is written as if it is "applying" *Roe*.[14]

Sometimes, however, we see explosive change—a paradigm shift—that can come from either the direction of ideas or practices. A new ideology or religious belief might dramatically affect practice; a radical change in practice—or a revolution itself—might dramatically affect our ideas. The American revolutionaries started out demanding the "rights of Englishmen" but in and through a political practice of rebellion discovered a belief in popular sovereignty. That belief, in turn, led them to initiate a new practice of constitutionalism, a radically different practice of law from that of the English common law.[15] We see the same sort of revolution during the New Deal: we cannot answer the question of whether the paradigm shift comes from a new idea of constitutionalism or the idea comes from the innovative political practices.[16] We should give up the idea of causation in either direction.

If ideas are not explained by the sociological analysis of causation, where do they come from? In particular, what are the sources of a theorist's claims? Here, Schmitt makes a simple point: ideas come from other ideas—not as the product of a deduction but rather as a free response to a proposition. For a third time, we are returning to an idea of freedom—not the freedom of the exception, not the freedom of the legal judgment, but the freedom of the proposition.

POLITICAL THEOLOGY AS FREE THOUGHT

Up to this point, the focus has been on the gap that is the locus and condition of the free act: the exception occupies a space outside the norm; the judgment fills the space between norm and application. However, we do not yet have an adequate understanding of how an act not determined by a norm can avoid appearing "unreasonable" or "arbitrary." Schmitt's existentialism needs to be grounded in some form of intellectual act that is neither deductively nor materially determined. We can find that ground by thinking about thought itself. Freedom in its political form is not something mysterious. It expresses in institutional form our experience of ourselves as free, thinking subjects who engage each other as such, even though we find ourselves embedded in structures of power that we cannot control. Even a slave knows what it is to have a conversation in which he or she speaks freely.

Judge and sovereign offer examples of the free act, an act that is neither determined by a norm nor arbitrary. The philosophical proposition is another. Neither the act nor the thought is predictable in advance, for neither follows as a matter of necessity—formal or causal—from its antecedents. That the sovereign and the philosopher are paradigmatically free men—and even in a competition of freedom—is an idea as old as Plato's speculations on the philosopher's role in the city. The philosopher and the sovereign are not in a causal relationship to each other—to think one depends upon the other would again be caricature—but both occupy the same structural position between past and future.

Both sovereign and philosopher can remove themselves from the predictable, ordinary path; both remain subjects—that is, operate with an autonomous will—even as they comprehend universal norms. Both, accordingly, can surprise us; they can say or do the exceptional. We might think of surprise as the psychological recognition of freedom, just as boredom signifies an absence of freedom. The point is not that philosophers should be kings or even that they should be Rousseauian legislators in the modern form of liberal theorists telling us what the laws should be. Indeed, to claim that philosophers should be kings is a proposition that assumes exactly the kind of causal relationship between ideas and practices that Schmitt rejects. Rather, both philosophy and politics turn on the possibility of freedom.

The distance between the free act and free thought turns out to be no distance at all. The disappearance of the distinction follows from the argument made above that practice is itself a form of symbolic expression. Accordingly, if we can understand the philosopher's activity, we will better understand the free decision in its political form. What, then, does the philosopher's freedom look like?

From the perspective of the ordinary biography of the philosopher, we must say, just as we say of the legal decision, it is as if the ideas come from nowhere. We call this "genius," "invention," or "inspiration." All of these are metaphors for what cannot be explained causally or deductively. We cannot predict the appearance of a philosophical idea. There is no distinction between predicting and having the idea, which is just another way of saying again that existence precedes essence. In truth, the appearance of an idea is only mysterious if we believe that every explanation must adopt one form or the other of causal reasoning. This is the wrong model, so we end up with mystery.

Ideas come from other ideas, not in the form of deduction or causation but just as in any conversation. This is the lesson that Plato draws from his experience of Socrates: philosophy begins in engaged discourse. Thus, one proposition will prompt another proposition in response. To speak freely is to respond to the other in a way that cannot be determined in advance. This is why conversation requires listening. To be a free agent is first of all to be able to say something new in response to another.[17] We discover our freedom every time we enter a conversation. Just as Wittgenstein argues that a private language is an incoherent idea, the idea of freedom would become incoherent for a wholly private person.[18] Of the last man, we will not be able to say whether he is free or determined. One consequence of this is that we often feel freest when we are most bound to another. The condition of free thought is not isolation from others. Rather, if freedom is realized in discursive engagement, then its condition is mutual recognition. Freedom is a practice we do together.

The philosopher steps into an ongoing conversation. He builds his theory from the elements of the conversation that he finds before him, but he "adds something"—just as was true in the theory of the judgment set forth in chapter 2. To be free is neither to report what has been said, nor simply to state what is implicit in what has been said. It is instead to respond. The response must be understood; it must make sense to the interlocutors. It is in this sense bound to what has already been said. It is situated, which means that it makes reference to what we might understand as the norm. But it must also be other than the norm or an application of the norm. Adding something, it is always exceptional. It most definitely is not what everyone would have said under the circumstances; it is rather what a particular subject actually says.

Characteristically, the philosophical project proceeds in two dimensions at once: genealogical and architectural. The philosopher must draw on the specific concepts that are passed on from one generation to another. Like the language he uses, concepts are an intellectual bequest from predecessors. Second, he sets these concepts into new relationships to each other. He juxtaposes meanings that had not previously been seen in such a relationship, whether a relationship of distinction or mutual support. Linking the subject to an object in the proposition is the paradigm of the free act. These two aspects of a philosophical discourse— genealogy and architecture—are just what Schmitt refers to when he speaks of "historical development [and] systematic structure" (36).

GENEALOGY AND INTERPRETATION

Ideas are not liquid assets to be put to any use one chooses. Rather, they bring with them remnants of their former meanings. It is as if one were building a cathedral with the remnants of a former church. The pieces one incorporates into the new structure will continue to reflect their former character. Nevertheless, by virtue of their placement in this new structure, we understand differently. We confront the new in and through the old, and vice versa. We do the same thing when we construct discursive propositions. Concepts have a kind of penumbra about them, carrying forward former resonances. We continue to hear in and through them an entire history of Western thought. Of course, they are constantly shedding some of those meanings, just as new meanings are attaching. Collective memory is no more forever than individual memory.

We are often surprised when we investigate the origins of a word. The surprise is not over lost meanings that are beyond recovery. Rather, the surprise is linked to clarification. We get a better purchase on a meaning of which we had only the vaguest intuition. Concepts don't carry these remnants in and by themselves, as if it were only a matter of being aware of etymology or of reading all of the lesser definitions in a dictionary entry. They carry these resonances as part of the larger system of thought and practice in which they have been embedded. Because a concept draws its strength from the entire social imaginary, the resonances it carries are felt before they are understood. Interpretation begins with bringing these resonances into more explicit awareness. This is, for example, the basis for Rawls's method of reaching for a "reflective equilibrium."[19]

Schmitt uses as his primary example of genealogical inquiry the concept of sovereignty. Sovereignty bears on its face its religious history: the "Lord our God" is the "sovereign of the universe."[20] Simultaneously, it refracts this web of meanings through a political history that placed the political sovereign in a direct relationship to God. The concept picks up the mystery of the sacral-monarch in Western history. It continues to carry a sense of mystery, of unity, of ultimate meaning, and of the power over life and death. That aura is transformed, not abandoned, as the sacral-monarch dies a violent death in revolution and the people take up the mantle of sovereignty. Popular sovereignty retains an air of majesty and mystery. Earlier elements of the concept are not lost, despite a move toward secularization, because they now create a set of expectations about the nation-state. The state remains a site of life and death; its territory remains sacred ground; its history is a narrative of the self-revelation of the popular sovereign. Someone or some institution will continue to decide for and against national existence. Those decisions are imagined as possible and their very possibility supports a continuing belief in sovereign power. Insofar as we maintain that web of beliefs, we find ourselves making sense of—indeed using—the concept of sovereignty. To the extent such decisions depend upon these concepts and narratives, they are matters in which we must have faith. That faith is "justified" when the decision works, that is, when others respond to it as a meaningful claim.

Even religious nonbelievers feel the pull of Western beliefs about the sacred. They understand what it means to speak of "hallowed ground," of the "ultimate sacrifice," or of "sacred honor." They may feel strangely moved by invocations of "we the people" as a transgenerational, collective subject—strange because they cannot explain this feeling to themselves. The belief is, nevertheless, maintained in a set of political practices, including rituals of collective memory. Were those meanings entirely lost, the concept of popular sovereignty might come to mean nothing more than the output of a democratic vote. Or, it might come to be seen as a conceptual anachronism that does more to confuse than to clarify our political thought, the view of a good number of contemporary political theorists.[21] Our own history can come to seem as strange to us as that of a distant culture.

Political theology begins with the observation that many of our important political concepts come to us as secularized versions of theological concepts. One aspect of the political-theological inquiry, accordingly, is genealogical. We want to expose the remnants of belief that are attached to our political concepts and maintained in our political practices. The only way to do that is by tracing the theological origins of those beliefs. Nevertheless, we are not passive recipients of a conceptual inheritance. We cannot do genealogy without thinking the concepts anew. We find meanings or we do not. When we do, they are our meanings to be elaborated in ways that make sense to us.

Ideas do not sustain themselves. They are sustained in the social imaginary; they are sustained only within entire networks of belief and practice. They are maintained as propositions, not as singular concepts, which is to say they are maintained within a framework of their possible deployment. Moreover, I don't just utter propositions. Propositions only make sense as a part of a narrative. The narratives, as I argued above, are themselves bound in reciprocal relationships to practices. Our position is always one of already finding meaning in the world. Each of us maintains multiple possible narratives. They are the diversity of accounts we might give of ourselves and our communities when asked to explain who we are, what we are doing, or where we are going. There is no single order to these narratives; there are no established limits. They are resources that can be combined, juxtaposed, or contrasted. They are used as much to explain our practices as to critique these practices.

Genealogy is a kind of metanarrative, the object of which is to trace resonances of meaning that we find ourselves attending to in thought and action. By constructing the metanarrative, of course, we emphasize certain resonances among multiple possible meanings. We cast our history one way rather than another. In doing so, we become that history.[22] We become it in a free act of appropriation. The genealogy of concepts is, in this sense, no different than the construction of any other historical narrative. This is always contested ground: Do we write a political history from above or below? Do we write social history or economic history? Do we write history as a struggle for religious freedom or as the emergence of cosmopolitanism? Writing the history of America, we become Americans of one sort rather than another.

ARCHITECTURE AND ANALOGY

Ideas come from ideas. There is not a fact of the matter, either in nature or society, that moves us independently of our ideas. This relationship among ideas is neither causal nor deductive. It is, instead, free, as in the free construction of one narrative rather than another. We do not derive our present way of thinking from previous ideas as if we were deriving a conclusion from a premise. We do not advance in history by working out the logical implications of our present beliefs. Without causal or deductive necessity, ideas come from other ideas through a process of analogical thinking.

The process of secularization to which Schmitt points in his analysis of modern political thought is just such a process of analogical reasoning. Holding to one proposition, we come to see some other proposition as similar or different. We make these connections—or we break connections—in a free act of thought. We are persuaded, not determined. We might better think of the nature of our beliefs as the product of rhetoric than of logic. Rhetoric's product is narrative, not proof. We believe that of which we are persuaded.[23] The boundaries of thought are the limits of our capacity to be persuaded.

Philosophy and politics are both forms of rhetoric because both are arguments made to and by free subjects. If they were not rhetorical performances, we would expect far more convergence over time, just as we find in a natural science. Philosophical and political debates are, instead, endless. Neither is something that we can get right and be done with. That both philosophy and politics may disdain the rhetorical description of themselves, that both make a claim to truth, tells us only about the way in which claims to truth operate in a practice of endless contestation. Historically, rhetoric begins as a practice of persuasion among free citizens of the Greek polis. It is the practice of political freedom. Western philosophy traces itself to exactly the same site and the same practices of discursive engagement. Just as the philosopher challenges the ruler as the paradigmatically free agent in Plato's work, so does philosophy challenge political rhetoric as the paradigm of free thought. We are never all that far from Plato when we do philosophy, a point exactly in line with Schmitt's thoughts about genealogy.

We are constantly framing our own lives, to ourselves and to others, as the subjects of a narrative. Our entire life becomes meaningful as a rhetorical performance. We think of ourselves as the subject of a novel of which we are both author and subject. We hear in the very word "novel," the suggestion of the new: our lives always appear to ourselves as the products of a free act. So does our political narrative frame the community's life as the product of a free act. The narrative structure makes it impossible to distinguish, from within, novel from history, fiction from fact, which is only to say that human facts are always the product of a free act. And, a free act is never a fact: it exists only as the subject of a narrative. Without the narrative, it would be arbitrary—inexplicable—rather than free.

The biblical narrative of human creation locates freedom at the origin of discourse: the serpent's speech is the first rhetorical performance.[24] Before there was narrative, there was no freedom. In this sense, freedom is dependent upon memory. When the narrative of a polity disappears, when all that we have left are broken remains of buildings and shards of artifacts, the human is reduced to the material. We can date and locate the remains but we have nothing to say about the life that gave them meaning. Existence precedes essence because until we offer a narrative of ourselves, there is no more meaning to our lives than that of those broken bits of a dead world.

To the method of genealogy, accordingly, we must add the method of analogy. Political theology must advance from genealogy to analogy.[25] For example, Schmitt says the exception "is analogous to the miracle in theology" (36). Further, "only by being aware of this analogy can we appreciate the manner in which the philosophical ideas of the state developed in the last centuries" (36). Analogy and genealogy intersect to offer a narrative. Philosophical inquiry is not set against our ordinary practices of belief and understanding. If the community were not open to the analogy between the miracle and the exception, the philosophical inquiry could hardly put in place that set of meanings. Imagine trying to introduce the concept of the exception into a system of artificial intelligence in which the idea of a miracle could appear only as a mistake.

To draw an analogy is to draw attention to a structure of meaning. When I analogize one concept to another—exception to miracle—I am seeing the world through a symbolic frame. It is a world that I can understand because it is already mine. This is exactly how we proceed when we explain the meaning of—interpret—any cultural production, whether a novel or an act of state.[26] We don't strip it of context but rather embed it by drawing the multiple analogies that situate the work in our world. Performing the act of interpretation, we do not discover truth. Rather, we make those truths when we freely see the world one way rather than another.

Consider Schmitt's example of the miracle. The miracle in theology sets forth a relationship between the particular and the universal, between sacred and secular time, and between the infinite and the finite. It suggests an extraordinary intervention—a presence and a willful decision—by a power other than those that operate in our ordinary lives. It has a spatial and a temporal dimension that represent points of intersection between the sacred and the profane. Establishing a site of sacred appearance, it reorders history and space. It can be beginning and end. It can set the community's narrative in a new direction; it is always memorable. The miracle touches on the idea of sacrifice, for the presence of the sacred always destroys some element of the finite. We associate the miraculous with the sacrifice of Isaac, the destruction of the Egyptians, the raising of Lazarus, or the resurrection of Christ. We might move from the micro level to the macro, arguing that all of creation is miraculous, by which we mean that it is all a showing forth of the infinite within the conditions of finitude. We cannot have miracles without belief in the personhood of God. Miracles are the free acts of a subject who happens to be a god. There are no miracles for the atheist. Finally, miracles don't appear without reason, even if they confound reason. The miracle announces a relationship to a sacred, caring God. Few are the miracles in which God intervenes to do injury to his chosen people. For this reason, *Job* is such a puzzling exception.[27]

To say that the exception is "analogous to the miracle" is to claim that our understanding of a political event draws on this web of meanings. There is not one analogy, but a multitude of similarities and distinctions to draw and redraw. We will emphasize some aspects and deemphasize others—that is what it means to be analogous rather than identical. The analogy only becomes possible if a sufficient number of elements of the theological outlook are already present in our political understandings. There must, for example, be a lawful regularity against which the exception stands; there must be a power outside the ordinary to which we look for a decision; there must be the possibility of the new erupting within the community's narrative. The community must be open to seeing itself and its history in this way. To say that "there must be" any of these elements actually goes too far. We can't know in advance whether any particular element is a necessary condition of the analogy. But without some combination of elements, the analogy will fail. It may fail—or succeed— at different points for different people. For this reason, drawing the analogy will as likely be the starting point of an argument as the answer to a question. The philosopher always stands at the very edge of possibility, calling attention to meanings—analogies—which remain possible or become possible but which have not yet entered our ordinary awareness. We cannot, in the end, tell whether he is recovering meaning or inventing it: genealogy and analogy are two aspects of one process of free thought.

To work out the meaning of a political concept, such as the exception, requires describing the web of meanings on both sides of the analogy. Until we take up that enterprise, we don't know how far we can push an analogy. We may, for example, come to conclude that we had it backward: it was our sense of the political exception that grounded our idea of the metaphysical miracle. Taking up this project of genealogical and analogical reasoning, we find that the deeper we go, the more we are exploring the boundaries of our own social imaginary. The test of an analogy, after all, is what is convincing to us. This is the sense in which philosophy—that combination of genealogical and analogical reasoning—is a rhetorical practice. It fails when it does not convince.

We draw upon these conceptual models as we move from one domain of experience to another—movement that is by analogy. For example, when we imagine that we are deliberating with respect to a personal decision, are we drawing upon an analogy to parliamentary arguments in which representatives actually debate prior to a vote? Or, does the analogy work in the other direction: do we model politics on an internal process of decision that each of us has experienced? Similarly, if we understand order to be the product of deliberate creation, then we will look to the idea of a creator in every domain of experience. Wherever we experience order, we will attribute it to a creator. We will constantly be offering variations on the theological argument from design. The position of the creator may be held by a mythical god, a political leader, a family patriarch, or a messianic leader. In each instance, it is the need to explain order that drives us back to the model of a creative power. If, on the other hand, we understand order to be the outward expression of internal regularities, that is, of what Aristotle called a "formal cause" or we call law, then we will dismiss efforts to locate a maker and seek instead to specify the internal logic of development. We will locate laws of the physical universe but also laws of history and laws of political order. Thus, Darwin undermines the argument from design: we can have order without an intentional act of design, law without a lawgiver. Evolutionary development, in its turn, becomes a rich source of analogical reasoning. The process is as endless as talk itself, for we are not reaching a truth but arguing with each other.[28]

The problem for thought is to be able to explain—to speak to—our experience. We simply have no way of establishing a hierarchy of explanations, as long as we recognize that ideas come from other ideas—not by deduction but by constructing analogies within and among an inherited set of concepts. We don't decide among models of order by asking which one is true in the sense of corresponding to some independent facts of the matter. We decide between them by using one or the other. Each becomes true as we use it to explain to ourselves and to convince others. Each becomes false when it no longer convinces.

The analogies that are convincing at any moment and with respect to a particular domain of experience cannot be simply those we derive by looking backward. Genealogical inquiry alone does not explain how and why we order experience as we do. To think otherwise would be like thinking that legal conclusions are determined by precedents or that historical narratives are stable and complete. Rather, precedents and existing narratives offer a rich array of possibilities that are constructed and reconstructed through the use of analogies. We don't even know what the precedents mean until they are deployed analogically in support of a present judgment. This is the method of common-law reasoning, which has become a universal method of judicial reasoning.[29] We resolve a legal problem by seeing it as analogous to a legal structure that we find already available to us. The "seeing it as" is the moment of freedom. There, we freely decide. Because it is a free act, there is inevitably the possibility of dissent, just as with other forms of argument there is always the possibility of disagreement.

John Dewey famously stated that facts don't carry their meanings on their faces.[30] Those meanings are there when we draw analogies one way rather than another. Disputes in the law are often disputes over what are the proper analogies to draw upon to give legal shape to facts. We might think of legal argument as a process of colonizing one area after another through the extension of analogies. There are, however, always counteranalogies that would move in different, if not opposite, directions. In American constitutional jurisprudence, for example, consider the pattern of extension of due process rights to what had been seen as government largess, the withdrawal of those rights, and then their renewed extension.[31] When we speak of a "controlling" precedent, we are pointing to a decision, not to a fact. Nothing controls until someone decides.

We go deeply wrong if we think that legal conclusions follow from premises as if they were logical deductions. We don't even have a minor premise to deploy until we have organized a fact pattern by using analogies. For example, consider how we go about determining whether a particular category—say, gender or sexual orientation—deserves "strict scrutiny" in American jurisprudence. We begin by asking whether it is "like" race, the paradigmatic category requiring such scrutiny. We pursue the inquiry by developing further analogies and disanalogies. We are "testing" the way in which we organize our beliefs and practices with respect to both the concept that we are considering and the category upon which we are drawing. In that pursuit, we are constantly reordering the web of meanings that are constitutive of our beliefs. Each iteration rewrites the narrative. In short, we construct an argument. Each step of that argument represents a decision, that is, a free act of thought. Only the naive believer thinks that just one argument can be made. There are as many arguments as there are possible analogies to draw and distinctions to be made. We know which is correct as a matter of law only after we know the decision.

While the materials out of which we construct arguments are inherited, the web of meanings that we sustain and the directions in which we move must be responsive to contemporary practices and beliefs. These contemporary elements often pull in conflicting directions, which is why we have disputes over how to think about an issue. If we focus on Schmitt's example of the exception, for example, we can understand why we would also be attracted to a contrary ideal of lawful regularity. This is a model that today may seem deeply rooted in the natural order, but before there was knowledge of the laws of nature there was an understanding of justice as treating like cases alike. We easily speak of justice as the rule of law, meaning that all are to be treated equally before the law. A regime of the exception may look less like a miracle and more like a failure of justice. This is not an idea that is a product of modern constitutionalism. Aristotle already struggled with the problem; it figured in the controversy between the scholastics and the nominalists. There is no uncontested space for the exception—that is, a space to which the concept of uniform justice cannot extend. There never has been. But the opposite is also true: we might think that the exception is a necessary condition of any social order because human relations can never be treated as if they were simply natural phenomena that repeat themselves. Every situation is different; each requires a response to the totality of circumstances. Here, our oldest model of order might be the prayer to an attentive God, that is, a God who is aware of and responsive to the fall of every sparrow. We want love as much as justice from such a God.[32]

We can't settle these disputes by arguing that one source of analogy—exception or equality—is right and the other wrong. We always find ourselves in the middle, making arguments to explain our situation, and finding that the arguments we make are contested by others. We find in ourselves the possibility of commitment to both analogies. To the extent that we care about the outcomes, we have no alternative but to take up the argument. We move at that point from the history of ideas to the practice of argument. It is the same with law: we can ask what nineteenth-century Americans meant by equality, we can try to get within their world of meaning. But if we ask what equality means as a matter of constitutional law, we must make an argument.

We understand the meaning of a concept only from within the circumstances of its possible uses. Arguments succeed when we find ourselves operating in the world with one set of meanings rather than another. In this sense, every genuinely philosophical inquiry is autobiographical, both as a theoretical and as a practical endeavor. To put analogy at the center of philosophy and decision at the center of analogy is to insist that philosophy is a practice of freedom for which we can be held accountable. Accountability should not mean that we send people to jail for their ideas; rather, it means that we should demand of them an explanation. We give them a chance to convince us, recognizing that we might be surprised by what they say.

The sociology of concepts, then, is not concerned with causal relations but with showing the manner in which "two spiritual but at the same time substantial identities" are related to each other (45). By "spiritual," we should mean no more than conceptual; by "substantial," no more than these concepts are already elements of a world of meaning.[33] The two identities are the respective objects of metaphysics and political theory. Their relationship is analogical. To take up the philosophical project in this way is to place at its foundation what we would today describe as the "social imaginary." Philosophy expands and historicizes the idea of the a priori.[34] It becomes a project of exploring the structure of the imagination, for our experience in thought and practice is always of a world of meanings, not of things-in-themselves or of abstract essences. A sociology of concepts stands at the intersection of cultural anthropology and the Kantian tradition of philosophy as critical inquiry. Schmitt's work has been rediscovered at the end of the twentieth century, at least in part, because we can see in him an early version of those forms of thought that were later developed by interdisciplinary theorists such as Foucault and Geertz.

SCHMITT AND THE POSTMODERN TURN

We can't know in the abstract at what point an analogy will fail. We come to know that point when we discover that a particular analogy does no work for us. To say of an event today, for example, that it was a miracle fails because in our understanding of the natural world, there are no longer sufficient elements of the web of theological meanings to sustain the analogy. With respect to the science of nature, lawful regularity has displaced every other possibility. It is a question of political theology to ask whether the failure of the idea of the miracle in the natural sciences has led to a more general failure such that the concept of the miraculous is no longer available to political thought. Surprisingly, Schmitt is inclined, at least some of the time, to answer this question in the affirmative, arguing that "the metaphysical image that a definite epoch forges of the world has the same structures as what the world immediately understands to be appropriate as a form of political organization" (46). A metaphysics that bans miracles in nature will go hand in hand with a political order that operates under law. Here, I part company from Schmitt. Of course, he is correct to insist that there are analogies to be drawn between metaphysics and politics, but he is wrong to think that an era's metaphysics sets the limits of political meanings. Such a claim is itself a form of reductionism; it is a caricature of exactly the sort he warns against.

Schmitt's openness to analogy is limited by a felt need for "coherence"—a concept that also has its own genealogy and analogical structure. He does not in any way share the postmodern appreciation of diversity, contingency, and bricolage.[35] Instead, his view about order is more characteristic of nineteenth-century German philosophy and indeed of the metaphysics of the Church. Thus, he makes a specific claim about the relationship among the multiple social imaginaries available to us. He sees them as falling into a kind of hierarchy, at the top of which is metaphysics or theology: "The juristic construction of the historical-political reality can find a concept whose structure is in accord with the structure of metaphysical concepts" (45–46). Political thought must find a place consistent with "the general state of consciousness" (45). This is a claim particularly convincing to someone who still lives within a social imaginary shaped by the idea of a created world, for at its base it is a claim about the normative character of the real: metaphysics merges with theology. A world created by a single God will exhibit a unity of order; it will have integrity. This was the foundation for centuries of natural law theory within the Church.[36]

Looking at the evolution of political forms, Schmitt sees a genealogy that draws directly on theological concepts, that is, on ideas of the sacred. Constructing a political order, either in fact or in theory, has meant to draw upon fundamental understandings of the nature of man, which necessarily includes beliefs about the normative order in which he stands. Schmitt speaks here in almost personal terms: "There is psychologically (and, from the point of view of a phenomenologist, phenomenologically as well) a complete identity. A continuous thread runs through the metaphysical, political, and sociological conceptions that postulate the sovereign as a personal unit and primeval creator" (47). This sense of identity, of a single thread, is certainly not limited to a particular metaphysical concept, that is, to a "primeval creator." As a structure of inquiry, political theology suggests exactly the contrary: every metaphysics will be linked phenomenologically to a political theory. The claim is not one of theoretical foundationalism, nor is it one of natural law. Rather, it is a claim about the nature and structure of the social imaginary: models of order imitate each other from the microcosm to the macrocosm. They must, since thought is built on analogies. This precisely cannot be a metaphysical claim, since it begins as an observation about the epochal character of political theologies. Metaphysics has already been historicized. It is, accordingly, a human science, not a natural science. Indeed, once historicized it is not a science at all but a rhetorical practice.

Schmitt has the phenomenology of theory right: theory explores the felt analogies by which we make sense of our world—all of it. He may also have been right that as long as we maintain a belief in a single, coherent metaphysics, that same model of order will inform our political thought. This "complete identity" of metaphysics and political theory, however, is no longer available, once it becomes possible to believe that there is no normative character to metaphysics at all. In a godless world, that is, a world with no normative significance whatsoever, there is nothing that nature has to teach us in thinking about how to order the political, except that it is entirely up to us. There is no political theory that follows from quantum mechanics; we may be beyond the boundaries of analogy. Indeed, quantum mechanics may be beyond the boundaries of the imagination altogether. One way to characterize contemporary physics is to say that we can know what we cannot imagine. If so, to draw a political analogy to today's metaphysics may have become impossible.

Of course, Schmitt does not think that theories of political order are simply applications of religious or metaphysical beliefs. That would not be a sociology of the concept but only the application of a concept. It would be theocracy, not political theology—"caricature" in the form of the causality of concepts. Yet, he does think that every epoch has its characteristic understanding of order: "metaphysics is the most intensive and the clearest expression of one epoch" (46). We can speak of an epoch of belief in an active, intervening god, of another epoch as one of belief in a Deist god who stands outside of the product of his creation, and of a third characterized by belief in immanent principles of evolution. We will bring our deepest beliefs about the way in which order operates in the world into our theories about the normative order of the state. Politics is always both a part of the larger order and a microcosm of that order. We read each through the other. Even today, it is not uncommon to see a defense of liberalism that begins with the idea that every individual possesses equal dignity because each is made in the "image of God."[37] On the other hand, we are just as likely to hear a defense of democracy claiming that it is "the expression of a relativistic and impersonal scientism" (49). Democracy follows both from belief in a caring God and from belief that there is no value apart from the choices of individuals. If democratic principles can follow from either proposition, then political thought has broken free of the unity of an epoch's theological conception—if there is any longer such a unity in our multicultural world. We are democratic first and then look for metaphysical analogies to support our political practices and beliefs. This is a statement about us, about the uses of analogy and the forms of persuasive rhetoric; it is not a claim for a new hierarchy as a descriptive truth of the world.

In the postmodern world, the sources of fundamental belief, the diversity of metaphysical approaches, the conflicts between religious and secular outlooks, and even the conflicts between the biological and physical sciences are just too many and too deep to think that we can offer a single theoretical model to characterize the epoch. Perhaps we should say that we live in a "postepochal" age. We find that people operate with diverse systems of belief, which do not fall into any coherent order. We have discovered that we can live with this incoherence. The center does not hold, but things do not fall apart.

While there is general agreement among secularists on the relativity of values across cultures, those same people find themselves to be strong believers in universal human rights. They are left unmoved by claims that one cannot coherently believe in universal rights without appealing to belief in a unitary God.[38] To such arguments, the refutation is in the practice: they do pursue a politics of universal human rights, and they do not share the religious belief. They have no overarching political theology that can fit the pieces of their political beliefs into a single, coherent framework. They simultaneously affirm the universality of rights and the particularity of meaning. Conflicts are resolved on an ad hoc basis, without any sense that there must be a single theory applied uniformly in every conflict. Everything is relative, until it is not.

Turning from politics to religion, we find the same kind of incoherence. Many religious believers are not capable of reconciling their faith with what they simultaneously believe about the scientific investigation of nature. They may be curious about the possibility of reconciliation of faith and science, but they are not incapacitated by the felt tension. Their practice escapes the boundaries of their ability to theorize. They literally cannot explain the life they lead. The same incoherence is true of contemporary philosophy. We are long past the point at which a philosopher has to put forward a theory that grounds his political ideas in his metaphysics. As a general matter, our political philosophers simply don't do metaphysics. They do not feel that they have to answer the question of the existence of God before they can say anything about the nature of political justice. To argue that such comprehensive coherence is the role of philosophy would be to say that philosophy is no longer possible.

Coherence is not only too heavy a demand to place upon ourselves, it was already too heavy a burden for Schmitt. His own work is actually a good demonstration of the incommensurabilities of belief systems. There is no single, grand analogy that orders the whole. Schmitt concedes that Kelsen's thought reflects the organizing ideas of the epoch: "Kelsen can conceive of democracy as the expression of a relativistic and impersonal scientism, [which] is in accord with the development of political theology and metaphysics in the nineteenth century" (49). Nevertheless, Schmitt rejects Kelsen's approach, insisting instead on the vitality of the concepts of sovereign decision and exception. That Kelsen's theory accords with the thought of the epoch is of interest to a sociology of the concept—ideas come from ideas—but Schmitt's own work marks a broader point: there are multiple forms of thought operating in contemporary Western political communities. The autonomy and completeness of law is one possible position; so is the idea of the sovereign as the power to decide upon the exception. The first two chapters of his book, after all, were about the centrality of the decision even to a regime organized under law.

Schmitt's varied attitudes toward Kelsen reflect a broader uncertainty over the object of political-theological inquiry: Is it directed at theory or ordinary belief? Is the question "why does Kelsen model his theory of law as he does"? Or, is it "how does Kelsen's theory stand with respect to a community of political beliefs and practices"? At times, Schmitt suggests that the former is exactly the project of political theology: it is metatheory. But we have no reason to go in that direction. The object of theology is not to explain the theory of the sacred but to bring theory and experience into contact. This is not because experience precedes conceptualization, as if fact precedes theory. Just the opposite. There is no moment of human experience that precedes its symbolic character. Theory is not different in kind from the ordinary understanding; philosophy begins in ordinary discourse. It is sustained self-reflection on that experience. It is a poor theology that fails to express a community's experience of the sacred, even if it is good at explaining why theological speculation takes the form that it does.

The same is true of political theology. A political theory that leaves no room for the decision is simply not a very good theory of politics, even if we can understand why such a philosophy might be put forward at a particular time. The theological element of politics is not the possession of the theorists. Thus, speaking of an earlier epoch, Schmitt writes, "it is a sociology of the concept of sovereignty when the historical-political status of the monarchy . . . is shown to correspond to the general state of consciousness that was characteristic of western Europeans at that time . . . .Monarchy thus becomes as self-evident in the consciousness of that period as democracy does in a later epoch" (45–46). Self-evident to the consciousness of the period is the critical concept. We believe in kings before we are confident in our theory of divine right. A theory, we might say, must feel right; it must express that which we already know. The very foundation of a methodology of the sociology of the concept rests on this idea, for the metaphysics of an era is always the most "self-evident" truth. It is self-evident in the way that all matters of faith are self-evident. Thus, the "truth" of a political theory has to be measured against how well it explains that which is self-evident. It is no accident that our own Declaration of Independence begins from truths held to be "self-evident."

Summary The real work of political theology, then, is done in giving a theoretical expression to those understandings that already inform a community's self-understanding. Even if we once could, we can no longer derive those concepts from the general tenor of thought of the epoch because there is no such thing. Rather, we must look to the way that political concepts are actually deployed in the life of the community. About those concepts we must ask both the genealogical and the architectural question. We ask where they come from and how they are held together in patterns of analogical coherence that maintain a universe of meaning. These are the forms of inquiry into the modern social imaginary. To take up these tasks is to offer an interpretation. To succeed is to persuade others.

What we find when we pursue these inquiries is that our political life remains deeply embedded in a web of conceptions that are theological in their origin and structure. Liberal political theory may express the theoretical tenor of our time, but it fails as a theory of political experience, at least as politics continues as a practice and source of meaning in the United States. Schmitt's critique of liberal theory remains apt: it is a political theory that lacks a conception of the political. In place of the political, it substitutes rational discourse, on the one hand, and interests, on the other.[39] Refusing to see the modern political community as a source of meanings that steps into the place of the sacred, liberal theory is forced to condemn much of our political practice as simply pathology, as if the aim of a political practice is to satisfy some normative theory. If we approach our political practices and beliefs as a culture, then we must ask about the nature and structure of the meanings it sustains for believers. To take up this inquiry is to turn to political theology.

CONCLUSION: POPULAR SOVEREIGNTY AGAIN

For countless Americans, sovereignty remains the critical element of their conception of the source and meaning of political life. The popular sovereign brought itself into being through a violent act of self-creation: the Revolution. The Constitution appears as a product of that sovereign actor, We the People. The popular sovereign sustained itself through the Civil War, and will continue to defend itself against enemies. The popular sovereign is understood as a collective, transtemporal subject in which all participate. It is the mystical corpus of the state, the source of ultimate meaning for citizens. The popular sovereign can always demand a life; it can demand of citizens that they kill and be killed for the state. The fundamental character of the relationship of citizen to sovereign is not contract—as in the social contract—but sacrifice. To be a citizen is to imagine the possibility of the sacrificial act. This is affirmed in the Pledge. The sacrificial moment appears as a kind of sacred violence: a force that realizes a transcendent meaning.[40]

Liberal theory simply misses the phenomenon of the political as it informs the life practices and beliefs of ordinary Americans; it misses their understanding of their relationship to national history and destiny. Only the state, not the church, can demand sacrifice of the person in the modern age. The structure of sacrifice as a giving up of the finite and taking on of the infinite remains just what it has always been. We don't experience the political order as merely the application of general laws arrived at through a democratic process. We also experience it as a source of ultimate meanings and a potential demand on life. At that moment, we see the decision for the exception, not the rule of law.

Arguably, we live at a moment when this set of beliefs is becoming more, not less, prevalent. The symbolic message of the terrorist is that political identity in and of itself is a matter of life and death. We can respond by appealing to concepts of sovereignty and sacrifice because these beliefs are available within the long history of Western practice. Taking them up, we take up as well their religious resonances. These conceptual materials are deployed in relationship to other concepts, that is, they are situated in new webs of meanings. The concepts are democratized and historicized; they are located in an historical narrative of colonial liberation and self-government. American political order, moreover, must link sovereignty to law, for whatever we believe about the sacrificial demand, we are equally committed to the idea that ours is a nation under law. This combination of ideas puts immense strain on the concept of the exception. To negotiate the relationship of law and exception becomes not just a problem for law but a problem for our understanding of ourselves in our relationship to the meaning of the political. There is no simple answer to this question. Liberal theory, however, fails even to see the problem. Precisely here, we need a political theology that traces the relationships—genealogical and analogical—among our patterns of belief.

Americans continue to maintain a set of beliefs not so different from those that Schmitt cites from Tocqueville's observations of nineteenth-century America: "in democratic thought the people hover about the entire political life of the state, just as God does above the world, as the cause and the end of all things, as the point from which everything emanates and to which everything returns" (49). Schmitt thought the clock was running out on these ideas: "It is true . . . that for some time the aftereffects of the idea of God remained recognizable" (49). About this, he was either too pessimistic or too optimistic. Political theology is not a normative enterprise that can tell us in which direction the mistake lay, although it can tell us that he was mistaken. The popular sovereign remains the efficient and the final cause—and I would say the formal and material cause—of American political identity.[41] A politics that is complete in itself, that wants only to realize its own truth, touches on the sacred.

4

ON THE COUNTERREVOLUTIONARY
PHILOSOPHY OF THE STATE

THIS IS THE MOST OBSCURE CHAPTER of an already obscure book.[1] It is hard to see how a discussion of the political implications of the views on original sin of a Spanish Catholic counterrevolutionary theorist from the first half of the nineteenth century has much to say to us. One easy reading simply assumes that Schmitt is turning to Donoso Cortes to offer a reactionary, political model as an alternative to Weimar constitutionalism. Whatever he may have thought personally of this idea, there is no such argument actually presented in this chapter. Indeed, the chapter seems to float off into abstraction, making no contact with contemporaneous events. It is instead concerned with the metaphysics implicit in paradigmatic positions of political theory—an inverse image of the previous chapter, which argued that the political theory of an epoch reflects its metaphysics. Schmitt seems more concerned with the relationship of the doctrine of original sin to political theory in general than he is with proposals for political or constitutional reform.

To explore this chapter in a useful way, we must once again ask what was the central idea that motivated Schmitt and whether it has a continuing relevance. Demanding that political theory confront the theological issue of original sin is simply not a useful way of approaching political theology today. Similarly, focusing on what it was that Donoso Cortes argued in response to the revolutions of 1848 is not the way to proceed. He is an example of a political theologian, not of the discipline of political theology as a contemporary intellectual project. The latter is an entirely secular field of inquiry, while the former expresses a sectarian endeavor that is no longer possible in the West. As I argued in the last chapter, a contemporary political theology traces the genealogy of political concepts and explores analogies between the political and the religious in the social imaginary. That inquiry is entirely independent of any beliefs about God and Church—or, for that matter, about original sin. Ironically, political theologians, just by virtue of their religious faith, may have a particularly difficult time adopting a political-theological perspective.

The critical and still compelling point of the chapter has nothing to do with the political implications of Catholic theology. Rather, it is the claim that differences among political theories rest not on different visions of programmatic reform or institutional organization; they arise out of radically different understandings of the nature of man. In the prior chapter, Schmitt's claim was that political theory is embedded in an epoch's deepest conceptions of the nature of order. This led to my investigation of genealogy and architecture as the manner in which the imagination structures experience. This chapter makes a similar point, arguing that political theories express our deepest conceptions of the meaning of human existence. Schmitt's target is what we might call the normative metaphysics of liberal political theory. That remains very relevant to us, although we have reason to question a good deal of his analysis.

The continuing importance of this question is implicit, for example, in the title of one of John Rawls's more famous essays, "Justice as Fairness: Political not Metaphysical."[2] Rawls's need to write the essay arose from the critique of liberalism mounted by modern communitarians, who made a charge of exactly the kind Schmitt has in mind. They challenged the idea of the subject—that is, of human nature—upon which Rawls built his theory of liberalism.[3] Rawls had hoped to develop a liberal theory broad enough to include all reasonable people, regardless of differences in their metaphysical points of view. The communitarians were not satisfied because Rawls's methodological individualism rests on contested assumptions about the boundaries of the self and the place of reason. Schmitt is less concerned with the boundary issue than with the place of reason. The point, however, is much the same: to criticize the understanding of the person upon which liberal theory rests. That understanding places reason at the foundation of its conception of the person as citizen.[4] Political theology places will, not reason, at the foundation.

POLITICS, FREEDOM, AND THE AESTHETICS OF CREATION

Despite the appearance of *Political Theology* as simply "four chapters" lacking a unifying theme, a deep and important theme has emerged in my confrontation with the text: freedom. My exploration has been an inquiry into the imaginative space of the free act, which is always an expression of will. In chapter 1, the free act was located in the sovereign decision for the exception. Analysis of that act required understanding how a decision can make reference to norms but not be determined by them. In chapter 2, the free act was located in the decision to apply a norm. In the juxtaposition of concrete facts and norms, there is always a gap filled by the free decision. This is the space of the contest of interpretations, a contest that can be resolved only by the decision. In chapter 3, the free act was located in the philosophical endeavor itself, that is, in thinking. All reflective thought, including political-theological inquiry, combines genealogy and analogy. Genealogy binds thought, while analogy sets it free. Together, they offer an analytic of the imagination.

In the three chapters, we have gone from freedom of the sovereign, to freedom of the judge, to freedom of the philosopher. We have moved from creation, to judgment, to thought. We are right to suspect that the freedom of thought analyzed in the figure of the philosopher is at the root of the other instances of freedom: the philosopher is everyman, for the capacity to formulate a new proposition—to express a new thought—defines the human condition. The free decision, wherever it appears, is grounded in free thought. Both liberal political theory and political theology see the connection of the citizen to the philosopher. Both understand philosophy as a form of discourse. One however, models the discourse on principle and deduction, the other on imagination and rhetoric.[5] One emphasizes reason, the other will. The argument has taken us back to the earliest conflict over the nature of philosophy—that between Socrates and the sophists.

The question that remains is not what are the implications of this theory of the will for political practice, but rather what are its implications for political theory. No work in fundamental philosophy can be normative if its object is to describe the human condition. That would be like pursuing the normative implications of a theory of language. Political theology as a philosophical practice tells us something about what the human condition is, not what it should be. Any dispute about particular norms occurs within the conditions of human action and judgment. Those conditions remain regardless of where we come out on controverted normative issues.

We can, however, ask of a political theory whether it has an adequate grasp of the nature of freedom. For Schmitt, that question comes down to asking whether a political theory has recognized the place of the decision. Without this, political theory fails phenomenologically; it is founded on a false metaphysics. That, however, tells us nothing about whether action taken in response to that theory would be just or unjust. The obscure dispute that is at the center of this chapter is exactly about the relationship of political theory to freedom.

For Kant, the question of freedom was that of how a subject could determine his own action in a causally determined world. The free subject, he thought, must give himself the principle of his action. He must be self-governing rather than governed from without. As a rational agent, moreover, his act cannot be arbitrary. He must act according a rule and the rule must express his nature as a rational agent. In the end, the free agent is determined in his actions by the very form of rationality: "Act only according to that maxim by which you can at the same time will that it should become a universal law."[6] Thus, the Kantian subject acts freely when he does what any rational agent should do, which is what any wholly rational agent would necessarily do. There is no personality at this point because the will is entirely filled by the universal rule. Subjectivity is always a problem from the moral point of view, for difference must be grounded in something other than reason. Personal difference does not show up in the formal sciences, such as mathematics. If moral action aspires to the universal, it must similarly approach the uniqueness of the individual with skepticism. Individual character is as irrelevant to morality as is the uniqueness of the body. Indeed, from the perspective of universal reason, individual character is tied to the body: its desires, interests, and circumstances.

The categorical imperative tells the agent to subordinate the will to the universal perspective of reason itself. The disappearance of the self in the act of willing the rule continues in contemporary political theory in the form, for example, of Rawls's veil of ignorance. That is a device for thinking of oneself as a subject shorn of the capacity to will anything in particular. Reason and will exactly coincide in the original position because imaging that position we find ourselves without knowledge about our particular interests or circumstances. Behind the veil, there is nothing to say that would not be said equally by everyone. To go behind the veil is to shed one's history, without which we have no character. It is the political equivalent of creation ex nihilo, but so then is every moral act according to Kant. For both Kant and Rawls, the capacity freely to act poses the problem of law, that is, of the need to subordinate the self to a universal rule. Freedom without law would, for both of them, be merely arbitrary.

This is not how Schmitt understands the problem of freedom. True, a free act can be neither arbitrary nor determined. The free act must have some relationship to norms, or else it would be arbitrary. It cannot, however, be determined by the norms, in which case it would not be free. On this view, the disappearance of the subject in the categorical imperative is as much an example of the lack of freedom as is the disappearance of the subject in a causally determined world. In neither case is there a place for the decision as the unique act of a person's will. But if the free act is not determined by cause or norm, how does freedom not collapse into mere arbitrariness? To avoid this, we must hold on to the idea that the free act is "not without reason," although it does not follow from any prior reason. To get to this idea, we need to focus on the nature of the will.[7]

Liberal theorists tend to collapse will into either reason or interest, producing the double origins of liberalism in deontological and utilitarian sources.[8] In neither direction, however, can we find an adequate ground for a theory of the free will. Political theology starts the analysis neither from the universal principle (the perspective of reason) nor from that of the subject's desire for an external object (the perspective of interest) but from that of the creative act. The idea of creation links the political decision simultaneously to God and to the artist. In each case, the problem is to understand how the subject's will can bring something new into existence. This sounds more mysterious than it is. Artistic creation has a relationship to norms, but it is not simply the deductive application of the norm. We don't create art by following a set of rules. Similarly, we cannot explain art by analyzing its causes—although once again there is some relationship to causal factors.

That there is no formal or physical necessity to aesthetic creation hardly renders it arbitrary. Nevertheless, it cannot be explained by reason or interest alone—or by both together. It requires that we develop a set of concepts adequate to the imagination of the creator. Of the imagination and its products, it makes as much sense to say that the universal is subordinate to the particular, as that the particular is subject to the universal. They are bound to each other in just the same way that the conversation modeled the free act in the last chapter. The critical ideas there were those of "response" and "surprise." A conversation is a reciprocal series of responsive surprises. The work of aesthetic creation is exactly the same. It is always a new beginning, but one that is responsive to what has come before. Absent the element of response, it would be arbitrary. Absent surprise, it would be a mechanical production. Every artistic work is an interpretation, which is exactly why we say of a work of art that it must itself be interpreted.

With respect to acts of the imagination, creative or discursive, we do not know the rule, the universal, until we confront the particular. This is the sense in which I argued earlier that the judicial decision determines the meaning of a precedent. Imagination is bound to particulars, but we see through the particular to an unlimited world of possibility. A successful work of art invites us to see differently; it literally recreates the world. The imagination, we often say, mediates between the particular and the universal. The particular alone would make no sense to us; the universal alone would allow no intervention by the subject.

The artist does not apply the universal, for there is nothing to apply until a meaning is set in the free act of creation. We speak of the artistic act of creation as an "interpretive performance." Artist and audience are equally creative, which is why the artist may be no better at explaining his work than a critic. We speak of artists as seized by a creative daimon or directed by a muse. What we mean is that they literally do not know how it is that they do what they do. They do not know because the imagination is not an expression of reason but of a free will. Again, this experience of creation is intuitively available to everyone: we do not know what we are going to say in a conversation until we say it. We are not applying a rule but imaginatively feeling our way.

The work of art demands of us—the audience—an interpretation. Metaphorically, we enter into a conversation with it; in fact, we enter into many conversations about it. The work becomes a site of contested interpretations, each of which has the capacity to lead us into an entire worldview. Even when we are confident we have understood the work, we never think that its production was determined by the logic of that interpretation. We remain, for example, open to the possibility that we will change our minds.

Each time we encounter the work, we can take up again the problem of interpretation from the very beginning. We cannot be sure that we will come out at the same place. This is because the work does not sustain itself as a thing in the world. Rather, it presents itself as constituted by a series of relationships to other works of the imagination. A change in interpretation anywhere in the network of meanings can be refracted in and through our engagement with the work. The work itself is engaged in a kind of conversation with us and with other works. We never lose sight of the particular, but the particular cannot supply its own meaning. Fully to explain its meaning would be to deny its aesthetic character, a problem with some forms of modern criticism.[9]

An act commensurate with human freedom must fill this middle range that represents an interchange between the universal and the particular. This domain is neither that of reason nor desire but of the imagination. A rational subject without an imagination would be no more free than an object wholly determined by the laws of nature. It would not see the domain of the possible but only of what must be. Aristotle's unmoved mover of the universe lacks imagination and can *do* nothing in particular. The Judeo-Christian God freely creates the world because he has will, the faculty by which the imagined moves from the possible to the actual. Thus, when God looks at his creation and judges it "good," he is reflecting on his work as an act of will informed by imagination. He is not merely executing an abstract plan. If God creates man in his image, meaning with imagination and will, then man too is characterized by his access to the possible. This is the story of the Fall, an act that would have been impossible for a subject determined only by rationality.

When work is nothing more than the application of a rule, we speak of "production," not creation. This is, for example, the labor of the production line. Following a set of directions is not an imaginative act. In productive work, the person can be replaced by a machine. Indeed, we welcome such advances because production always has about it a sense of repetition and thus of drudgery.[10] Creative—that is, aesthetic—production is always unique exactly because it does not follow from a norm, even though it has a relationship to norms. That relationship is interpretative. Aesthetic production is an act of meaning that is realized in a decision. An artist who could not decide would produce nothing. Authors know this experience as "writer's block," but the same indecision can block any form of creativity, including political action.

Unlike deduction or mechanical production, the decision always combines creation and destruction: the willed act excludes some possibilities, even as it realizes others. Freedom is choice, and choice is always for and against. For this reason as well, the creative act can always fail. If we see only destruction, we will lose sight of the value of freedom. The more radical the creative act, the more likely it will be condemned by many as mere destruction. We intuitively grasp that freedom has costs. Aesthetic production is never just "fun"; it always has an element of suffering. This is not the suffering of labor. Rather, it is the suffering that comes with the constant need to decide, to will one end against others. The more creative the artist, the more he lives on the edge. Not knowing how he does what he does, he can never be sure he can do it again.

We cannot help but see the artist as free agent in and through the object of his creation. If we fail to see the free subject, we will look for different—nonaesthetic—explanations of the coming into being of the object. These may be psychological or social causes; we may dismiss the work as merely derivative.[11] If politics is a product of creative action, then we must see through it to an agent. More precisely, seeing the polity as the result of free action, we see as well the sovereign whose free act it is. Thus, seeing the Constitution as the product of a free political act, we see the popular sovereign as its author. Conversely, if we fail to see a sovereign subject, then we will not see the political order as the product of a free act. This is a politics in which no one can locate a point of decision, even while laws seems to proliferate.[12] If we see no agent making a decision, then we will also fail to see the multiplicity of interpretive possibilities.[13] Rulings will look as if they are the inevitable application of a norm—just the self-understanding of the bureaucrat.

The sovereign has just one faculty: will. We do not speak of the popular sovereign knowing or wanting but only willing. It wills the nation into existence, just as the sovereign god willed the cosmos into existence, and just as the artist wills the aesthetic object into existence. In all these cases, we don't start from a position in which we see the actor and then discover the products of his free acts. Someone who claimed to be an artist but produced nothing would be expressing a meaningless statement. Again, there is no essence before existence. We start from a perception of the product and infer the presence of the free subject. The space between object and subject is the domain of the imagination; it is traversed in one direction by interpretation and in the other by the free act of creation.

Politics as a performance of freedom fails when we cannot see the state itself as a product of our own acts. To see the state as the product of popular sovereignty and the self as a participant in the sovereign is the fundamental narrative of political freedom in the postrevolutionary age. Again, creation and interpretation are bound together. There is no longer a distinction to be made between artist and audience. Reading the state as the product of our own freedom, we experience its claim on us as legitimate. As the realization of the self's freedom, a legitimate political practice is incompatible with coercion or indifference. Legitimacy, however, is neither a necessary condition of justice nor a substitute for justice. But correspondingly, justice is not a substitute for legitimacy.

The difference between positive political science and political theology is well captured in their differing attitudes toward this imaginative inference of a sovereign who creates and sustains the state. Political science views this as yet another example of a false argument from design: that political order exists no more supports an inference of sovereign creation than does the existence of natural order support an inference of God's existence. Political theology, on the other hand, finds the inference to be a form of faith that grounds political experience. When we follow the argument in this direction, we see exactly the broader point of Schmitt's chapter: political theories do indeed contain an implicit metaphysics. We can see the state as a product of a free act—our own—or we can see it as a structure of power that acts upon us. If we take up the former interpretation, we write a narrative of creation: the myth of popular sovereignty. If we take up the latter, we ask who has succeeded and who has failed in the marketplace of political power.

The sovereign act of will that is political creation is simultaneously universal and particular. If we view the state as legal order, we see the universal. There is nothing particular about legal ideas of equality or due process. This is the great promise of human rights as legal rights. If we view it as a sovereign entity, we see the particular.[14] Our borders and our history belong uniquely to a national narrative. The sovereign wills into being the rule of law. This is the intersection of the particular and the universal on the grandest scale short of cosmological creation.

LIBERAL THEORY OR LIBERAL STATES?

When it is not obscure, there is much in this chapter that is just wrong. While it is important to recognize that at least an inchoate, philosophical idea of the nature of man is at stake in political theory, Schmitt focuses immediately on the extremes, as if every political theory must answer the ultimate theological question of the goodness or sinfulness of man: "Every political idea in one way or another takes a position on the 'nature' of man and presupposes that he is either 'by nature good' or 'by nature evil'" (56). Surely, there is much room in-between: what man is by nature may be less relevant than what he can become under different circumstances. The pressure of the ultimate metaphysical question, in turn, pushes Schmitt to see political positions as tending toward extremes: anarchy or dictatorship. The former would allow the essential goodness of man to stand free of the corrupting influences of power. The latter would deploy authority to allow no space for the expression of man's sinful nature. Again, we have no reason to think that this is the only choice available to us or that all intermediate positions must move toward the extremes. This has not been our experience. Worse, posing the question in this form seems to deny the very foundation of liberal political theory, which is the belief that a political order can be designed around an idea of justice that is acceptable to those who take very different—even opposing—positions on these theological questions.

Looking at liberalism through his framework of extremes, Schmitt sees an unstable and untenable effort to avoid decision of the ultimate question, that is, the question of good or evil. Liberalism, he charges, wants to work everything out: "The essence of liberalism is negotiation, a cautious half measure, in the hope that the definitive dispute, the decisive bloody battle, can be transformed into a parliamentary debate and permit the decision to be suspended forever in an everlasting discussion" (63). Liberalism is indeed cautious, believing that all men can behave well or poorly, that justice is a human virtue, and that political structures can be made more or less well to respond to the weaknesses that even good men bring with them to political power. This caution produces the familiar institutions of liberal constitutionalism: separation of powers, judicial review, electoral contests, a doctrine of rights, and party competition. Today, these qualities of institutionalized caution are likely to appear among liberalism's virtues, not its weaknesses.[15]

Liberal political structures are justified on the ground that men are easily corrupted by their self-interests. To this observation of human nature, liberal theory brings a faith that men—at least enough of them—can be persuaded by rational argument to act on the common good. Minimally, they can be persuaded at the moment that they are designing their political institutions, that is, framing the basic rules and structure of government.[16] Liberals are hardly attracted to the position of anarchy that Schmitt suggests must be the endpoint of any theory that assumes that men are not irredeemably fallen. Just the opposite, liberals believe that without political structure men will fall to temptation.

Liberals do believe that men are sufficiently rational and have sufficient self-understanding to put in place institutions designed to check their own self-interested tendencies. Nevertheless, they also believe that the institutions we have are never quite up to the task of neutralizing the effects of factional interests on the formation of policy. The institutions fail because they are subject to capture by just those self-interests that they are meant to control.[17] Liberal politics is, for this reason, a ceaseless cycle of reform as self-interest manifests itself and must be displaced yet again by appeals to public reason. Liberal institutions are, in this sense, designed to be self-correcting. Because reform is always on its agenda, liberalism stands in constant need of a clear expression of an ideal measure. Liberal theory responds by invoking yet more discourse—this time of the right sort, whether behind Rawls's veil of ignorance or in pursuit of Habermas's ideal speech conditions.

Schmitt's focus on the unresolved theological issue can, however, serve as a metonym for a whole series of unresolved issues characteristic of liberalism. Looking at the liberal politics of his age, he writes:

> Although the liberal bourgeoisie wanted a god, its god could not become active; it wanted a monarch, but he had to be powerless; it demanded freedom and equality but limited voting rights to the propertied classes in order to ensure the influence of education and property on legislation, as if education and property entitled that class to repress the poor and uneducated; it abolished the aristocracy of blood and family but permitted the impudent rule of the moneyed aristocracy; it wanted neither the sovereignty of the king nor that of the people. What did it actually want? (59–60)

Some of this remains true, but for the most part other points of indecision have arisen. Thinking of our own liberal constitutionalism, we see, for example, a regime that wants a strong president yet insists simultaneously on legislative supremacy, and a system that asserts the democratic grounding of political legitimacy but is equally committed to judicial review. Liberals endlessly dispute whether illiberal views can be excluded from the public debate, or whether liberty can be allowed to jeopardize equality. More broadly, we confront the moral demand for global justice and the particular demands for care of our local communities. What do we actually want?

Liberalism as a political form of reflection simply does not have the resources to resolve these tensions, because they arise at the point at which the necessities of political existence intersect with a normative theory of discursive rationality. They arise at the point of intersection of will and reason. Even a liberal state must first create and then maintain itself as a political formation. If politics has its origins in the decision, then liberals will never quite understand the ground of their own state. They constantly make the mistake of believing that we can resolve conflict by properly structuring the terms of conversation to include all relevant parties. As in the Paris Peace talks of the 1970s, they think that if we can get the design of the table right, then agreement will follow.

Liberalism's political sin is the belief that it can always be inclusive because talk will lead to understanding, and understanding to agreement. Sometimes more talk just leads to more disagreement. There is no misunderstanding between our own conservatives and liberals or religious believers and secular humanists. We don't resolve these conflicts by "talking about our differences." Of course, not every political conflict leads to violence, and sometimes conversation does avoid violent conflict. But we are mistaken if we think that the resolution of such conflictual discourse is achieved when each side comes to see the same truth, as if they all agree on the proof of a mathematical proposition. More often, political conversation succeeds when each side compromises, not when all sides reach the end of their differences.

Compromise preserves the possibility of return to the issue not because we must remain open to discursive challenges to legitimacy, but because, as a decision, a compromise can always be reopened through a new decision. Thus, we cannot know in advance whether a compromise will hold or whether it will become the starting point for a new round of conflict. If compromise is based on a judgment about costs and benefits, about the risks of violence and the likelihood of success, these calculations can change over time. Schmitt, looking at Weimar, sees in such compromise the threat of violence. He believes, therefore, in an urgent need for coherence and unity. We are more likely to speak of creative energies that come from such tensions.

Of course, to appreciate the creative possibilities of disagreement, we must already believe that the political disputes that arise within our community are entirely unlikely to break out into violence. We no longer imagine violence among ourselves as a political possibility. We don't worry about the possibility of a putsch. Once we have decided for friendship—political or familial—we can argue endlessly. The Jews have talked for millennia with neither agreement nor civil warfare. In Schmitt's terms, we cannot imagine fellow citizens as "enemies." This is the set of circumstances that allows us to see a failure to resolve political disagreement as a virtue, not a danger. For this same reason, when we look at similar tensions between ourselves and noncitizens, we are less likely to think that conflict is creative and more likely to think it dangerous. Just at the point at which violence is imagined as a possibility, we are not likely to adopt the liberal enthusiasm for diversity. We talk, then, in the shadow of force—exactly the kind of nonideal speech situation that liberal theory disavows.

Schmitt seems to have agreed with Donoso Cortes's description of bourgeois liberals as "a class that shifts all political activity onto the plane of conversation in the press and parliament" and is, therefore, "no match for social conflict" (59). This turned out to be just false. Internally, a liberal political order can be as stable as any other; externally, liberal polities have shown themselves quite capable of defending themselves. The really interesting question, which Schmitt never reaches, is whether the stability of the liberal state rests on its liberalism. If Schmitt is right that every political order rests on the decision, then liberal theory cannot offer an adequate account of the foundation of the liberal state. Precisely because liberal states are, first of all, sovereign states, their liberalism remains incommensurate with their actual political commitments. This is one way of understanding why liberal theorists are never happy with the liberal state. The theory and the practice of liberalism can never coincide—or, at least, they cannot coincide within the boundaries of the nation-state. For this reason, liberal theorists seem always to be on their way to cosmopolitanism.

Liberal theory does not want to take a position on the nature of the good, which does indeed mean that it has no view on the essential goodness or evil of man. It seeks to construct a political order independent of such metaphysical questions—although, as I argued above, it surely does rely on a metaphysics of the individual and of reason. It makes no difference to the theoretical constructions of liberalism whether the political order is to occupy heaven or hell. Kant captured this precisely in saying that the task of political theory is to design a just order that can operate even among a race of devils.[18] Today, instead of hell, we would speak of the prisoner's dilemma, but the point is same: political order is exogenous to individual interests, including the individual's interest in the state of his soul. Liberals, however, have hardly been rendered immobile by their failure to resolve the theological issue. Western liberalism as a political practice has been no less a fighting faith than other ideologies.[19] Schmitt misjudged the forces and direction of Western history. He attributed too much power to theory—perhaps the philosopher's mistake. Thus, Schmitt is not much of a guide for understanding the liberal polity. Does he do better as an analyst of liberal political theory?

LIBERAL THEORY AND THE REVOLUTIONARY LEGACY

Rather than think of this as a chapter about original sin, we do better approaching it as a chapter about authenticity: the normative claim characteristic of existentialism and of modernity more broadly.[20] Is this a concept that we can usefully extend from the individual to the polity? That is, can we speak of a political experience as one that has the virtue of authenticity or the vice of bad faith? Can we think of an entire political order as more or less authentic? Is at least part of the point of political theory not just to formulate a concept of justice but to illuminate from within the possibility of political authenticity? This is one way to think about existentialism as form of philosophical inquiry: it aims to be both a theory and practice of authenticity.

Schmitt would not be alone in the early part of the twentieth century in thinking that there is a connection between a revolutionary politics and claims of authenticity.[21] Counterrevolutionary philosophy, to which the chapter title refers, is less a matter of challenging the concept of justice underlying a revolutionary philosophy than of challenging the existential status of revolution itself. This is why we find the focus on original sin. If revolution claims to be an experience of authenticity, then the counterrevolutionary response is that such an experience cannot bear the weight of man's sinful nature. On this view, the experience of revolutionary authenticity is really one of sin—of pride—because without God man cannot overcome his fallen condition. The belief in the possibility of revolutionary self-creation is not just likely to lead to evil acts, it is the very nature of evil. Thinking ourselves the embodiment of the authentic voice of the people, we will find ourselves pursuing not the virtue of charity but the vice of terror.

Revolution is an entirely modern concept, not because of its ideal of justice but because of its relationship to popular sovereignty. It is not simply an exchange of one party for another or of one faction for another. A coup is not a revolution. Neither is mob violence, even if it destroys the existing political leadership. From the American and French experiences onward, revolution begins with the concept of popular sovereignty: revolution transfers sovereignty from the body of the king to that of the citizens. Whatever it was that the particular individual became through the ritual of coronation, the people now become through the experience of revolution. The object of that becoming is to take on the double aspect—the "two bodies"—of sovereignty. The finite body becomes a point for the revelation of the sacred. Revolution, accordingly, is a matter of "presence." This is the source of its claim of authenticity. To speak about this, we have to turn to a theological vocabulary.

Every revolution claims political power in the name of a sovereign people. The outcome of revolution is always a "people's republic," regardless of the particular organization of government that emerges. This transfer of sovereignty—the destruction of one sovereign and the appearance a new sovereign entity—constitutes a break in national history. History begins again. That which happened before the revolution is reread as "preparation for" or "the road to" revolution; that which comes after holds forth the revolutionary truth as its source. This is the sense in which revolution shows itself as a secularized form of revelation. It is always miraculous.[22] To be as a part of the revolution is to experience the mystical corpus of the sovereign. No such experience is possible without a leap of faith. There is no proof of the people's presence apart from the experience itself.

Without a sovereign showing forth, there can be no revolution. The sovereign that shows itself in the modern age is always the people. Revolution is never partial; it is whole and complete. It demands of everyone that they *be* as the people.[23] The morality of revolution is not justice but rather authenticity, which we can understand as a unity of being and meaning. It is the phenomenological appearance of the proposition I have repeated in each chapter: existence before essence. The virtue of revolution is the fact—that is, the experience—of revolution. A postrevolutionary era is, for this reason, inevitably felt as a moral failure. It is the point at which the people again become ordinary subjects with particular concerns of family, profession, and well-being. They may be more just than their revolutionary parents, but they have literally stopped dwelling with the gods.

To pass into the imagination of revolution, there need not be actual violence, but there must be the threat of violence and an expressed willingness to sacrifice. A nonviolent revolution is a misnomer. A revolutionary movement can decline to exercise violence against others, but it must be willing to suffer violence. It must embrace the possibility of sacrifice, for finitude itself is on offer. A transition of political form that was entirely peaceful, using only the vote with no threat of violence, would not be seen as a revolution. It would only be successful reform. The American civil rights movement stands in the revolutionary tradition because of its embrace of sacrifice, even as it took up a strategy of nonviolence.[24] Gandhi's was a nonviolent revolution, but it too was steeped in self-sacrifice.[25] The recent color revolutions of Eastern Europe, as well, were suffused with expressions of a willingness to suffer sacrificial violence, even if, for the most part, the threats did not seriously materialize. When we confuse nonviolence with "peaceful" change through the ballot box, we have forgotten the meaning of revolution. The difference is between that which we do out of interest and that which we do out of love. Interest is not necessarily unjust and love is not necessarily just.

Revolution, accordingly, refers not to a change in policy—radical or otherwise—but to a new way of being as a part of the polity. Revolutions bind the future just as long as they are imagined as action by the popular sovereign—a transtemporal, collective subject. This concept of sovereignty is incomprehensible if stripped of its theological origins. That sovereignty could be directly instantiated in any and every citizen—unmediated by the kingly body—was surely among the deepest changes marking the emergence of a modern social imaginary. It was a change as deep as the transformation of the locus of the mystical body of Christ in the Protestant Reformation. It is the political form of this same change of the locus and character of the sacred. In both cases, the relationship of the individual to the sacred is now direct (without any intermediate functionary), mystical (outside of ordinary space and time), and of ultimate significance (a value beyond life itself). None of this is a matter of reason; all of it is a matter of will, imagination, and faith.

The postrevolutionary state maintains this narrative of direct action by the popular sovereign, the people. Belief in the popular sovereign sustains a faith in the revolution as a kind of sacred presence. Its authenticity remains separate from its justice. Authenticity can support an idea of legitimacy quite independent of justice.[26] America's revolution, for example, preserved the injustice of slavery. For some—especially the victims—this injustice made it impossible to see the Revolution as an authentic act of popular sovereignty. But many could recognize the injustice and still affirm the authenticity of the Revolution as an act of popular sovereignty and the legitimacy of the law that has its origin in this act.

This does not mean that revolution is inattentive to an ideal of justice. Neither, of course, was a virtuous king. Nor does it mean that claims of justice are always subordinate to those of authenticity. Generally, we are bound to the sovereign despite its multiple failures to bring about justice.[27] We seek to reform unjust law rather than overthrow the political order in a new revolutionary act—that is, until the moment of revolution actually arrives. A nation that begins in revolution always stands in danger of becoming fundamentally conservative, for its legitimacy depends upon the preservation of a relationship to that originating act of self-creation. America is just such a conservative revolutionary state.

Liberalism is the dominant political theory of modernity, but it is not commensurate with the revolutionary foundation of the modern state. That originating act creates the distinction between authenticity and justice. Liberal theory, however, understands revolution only as a remedy for injustice; it is a matter of rights and their enforcement. The theory has no way to theorize the experience of authenticity, which may be legitimate even as it is unjust.

Liberal political theory, accordingly, has no place for sovereignty but only for law. Without the sovereign, liberal theorists understand a just law to be a legitimate law. But even of just laws, we can and do ask, "Whose laws are they?" Is this not the question that Europeans ask of the output of Brussels? It is the same question Americans ask of international law.[28] A law becomes our own when we recognize the free act that brings it into being as our own. That free act encompasses the legal order as a whole (chapter 1) and the particular judgment that gives force to one interpretation rather than another (chapter 2). Neither form of free action is possible without free thought (chapter 3).

The puzzle is how Western nation-states moved from the experience of revolution to the theory of liberalism, from an experience of an authentic politics to a theory of justice.[29] In truth, this is no movement at all, for justice is already there at the origins. Locating revolution in popular sovereignty specifies only the actor, not the scheme of governmental organization or the character of the law that is the product of the people's self-creation. The sovereign decision must have a content, even if it does not follow from that content. The sovereign must decide for something. It must create government and law, just as God must create a world of one sort rather than another. The shape of government that emerges in the course of a revolution is necessarily related to contemporary understandings of justice and of institutional design. Both of these stand as universal to the particularity of the sovereign decision. We go wrong, however, in thinking of that decision as if it were only the application of the universal. The decision makes reference to the norms but is not determined by the norms.

The revolutionary voice takes for granted that it speaks in the name of the popular sovereign. Speaking in the name of the people, however, hardly specifies the political path any more than claiming to be an artist determines the character of the work of art. Any particular proposal or plan must still be defended by reference to the norm of justice because justice is the measure that we bring to law. Justice, in other words, emerges just at the point that revolution transforms itself into law. The sacrificial act of revolution must transform itself into a constitutional text; exception suspends law, but does so always on the way to law.

Political Theology began with an observation, "Sovereign is he who decides on the exception." The popular sovereign voices revolutionary presence just at the moment that it can effectively decide on the exception. It claims the power to decide in expressing a willingness to sacrifice. Sacrifice and decision are not themselves expressions of liberal theory, for neither is a matter of reason. Nevertheless, the legacy of revolution in the West is liberalism. This is why liberalism as a political practice remains a fighting faith, that is, a matter of life and death.

The sovereign act, like other forms of revelatory experience, only achieves a stable place by transforming itself. To remember God's presence is not the same as to experience God's presence; to remember love is not the same as to be in love. At moments of revelation, we stand within the *mysterium tremendum*. Nothing can be more exhilarating or more threatening than to find oneself within a revolution. Sacrifice is the medium of sovereign presence. Permanent revolution is always a terrifying idea for just this reason. To succeed, revolution must transform itself into a regular political form, that is, it must produce a constitution. That constitution binds as long as it is seen as a remnant of revolution. To see through the constitution to the popular sovereign whose act it records is what makes it literally *our* constitution, despite the fact that we, as finite individuals, neither wrote it nor approved it. This is not a matter of "implicit consent" but of a social imaginary that grounds faith. The constitution claims us not because it is just—although we want it to be just—but because it is a remnant of a politics of authenticity that we still imagine as our own.

Constitutional governance in the United States is less about justice than it is about maintaining this belief in popular sovereignty: if the belief fails, constitutionalism can easily become governance by the dead hand of the past. Or worse, decisions of the Supreme Court in the name of the Constitution seem simply to be arbitrary and capricious actions by an entrenched minority: they are neither just nor ours. The Constitution aims for the same existential status as the Bible: it shows forth the sacred even as it marks the retreat of the sacred. This is a very old idea: law is the miraculous product of God's will that binds even after God has withdrawn. Following the law is the way in which ordinary people in ordinary times maintain contact with the sacred, once they can no longer speak directly to God. Is this not what the Old Testament prophets said? This is the tradition that was carried forward to the new world by the Puritans, that informed the first political-religious communities here, and that continues to inform our political imagination through faith in popular sovereignty and reverence for law.[30]

A modern revolution can normalize the transcendent experience of popular sovereignty in just one way. The logic of modern revolution, as deployed in the United States and France, represents the deliberate imposition of the order of reason on the people, by the people themselves. In a political revolution, the people always make a claim to the universal: they bring down the old in the name of justice; they construct a new order informed by justice. Revolutionaries believe in their own virtue. Even terror is carried out in the pursuit of justice. This is the point of contact between popular sovereignty and political philosophy, between Reformation and Enlightenment. A claim for a revelatory experience that made no reference to justice would not be a political claim at all. It might be personal, as in the nature of romantic love, or it might be religious, as in forms of fundamentalism. No doubt some mass movements founded on charismatic leadership approach this, but they are distinguished by their resistance to normalization.

Revolution promises a new covenant to be sure, but that covenant can refer only to the people's own act of self-formation. It is the people's acknowledgment of "self-evident" truths. Modern revolution is never simply an expression of ethnic nationalism: it is always self-formation on the way to justice. Can we even imagine a revolutionary rhetoric stripped of the claim to justice? Thus, the postrevolutionary conception of the constitution is that it is the product of political science as much as of popular action. Lincoln grasped this when he linked the idea of government by the people to the idea of a nation "dedicated to a proposition." Not just the enthusiasm but the wisdom of revolution survives in the popular imagination. Indeed, the wisdom is intended to last well after the enthusiasm dies away. The enthusiasm may cycle episodically through national history, but justice is to endure.

Accordingly, modern revolution becomes possible only with the birth of the science of politics. That science spans "self-evident" truths, a doctrine of rights, and institutional design, a doctrine of limited power. These revolutions begin only with a sovereign decision, but they leave in their place an understanding of politics as a field for the application of reason. They are moments of reason and will, in which there is an indissolvable connection between the two. The revolutionary speaks as the embodied voice of the popular sovereign, but he also speaks with the purity of reason, for modern revolutions are Enlightenment projects. Conceptually, they are made possible by the idea that a people can re-form itself on the basis of reason. Practically, they arise with a claim of injustice directed at an existing regime.

Injustice is now understood as an offense to universal principles, that is, to "self-evident truth." All citizens, because they have reason, can identify the injustice; all can order their own actions in light of what justice demands. A person incapable of self-ordering is a slave. Revolution proclaims that the existing conditions amount to slavery and that the people will no longer be slaves. This is the discourse that links the eighteenth-century American Revolution to the twentieth-century revolutions of decolonization. It links both, of course, to the narrative of Exodus as well: there too the theme of justice is inseparable from that of sacred presence. Justice, however, was not yet a project of enlightened reason.

Modern revolutions characteristically seek to remake the state to cure injustice. This ambition is possible because political institutions are now understood to be objects of technical construction, which can be crafted in a better or worse manner. The measure is to be found in the science of politics. Again, in the American and French experience, that science is no longer the unique possession of the "legislator," a Solon like figure that still inhabits Rousseau's thoughts, for example.[31] Rather, the new science of politics is available to everyone. Republics, we are told by Montesquieu, require virtuous citizens more than other forms of government.[32] There is a new equation of self-regulation with political action. Revolution succeeds when persons form themselves to be the citizens required in the republic of reason: moral and political virtue coincide in the modern idea of the citizen.[33]

Before the Reformation there could be no such thing as popular revolution, only the shift of power from one class or group to another. After the Enlightenment, revolutions must claim to throw off the irrational and put in place the truth of reason. The idea that politics can be a kind of applied science is the particular target of conservative thought, just as the claim that the people can bear the sovereign presence is the target of counterrevolutionary thought. The former was Burke's great complaint against the French Revolution. Politics, he thought, cannot be the product of an abstract science but is rather the product of the slow, organic growth of a community—its institutions, practices, and customary beliefs.[34] The latter is the target of Donoso Cortes, who is Schmitt's interlocutor in this chapter.

The Western revolutionary legacy is liberal constitutionalism. Modern constitutions have been liberal because modern political thought has been liberal. Theory had been moving in this direction before the revolutions arrived. There was, in fact, no necessary connection between liberalism as a theory of the just order of the state and revolution as an experience of popular sovereignty. Nations without revolutions moved along the same liberal track: consider Canada, which shares a broadly liberal political philosophy with the United States but has had no experience of popular revolution. Even Tocqueville, who deeply appreciated the democratic, revolutionary quality of the United States, was well aware that the ancien régime of France had been moving in the direction mapped out by liberal theory.[35] Liberalism's connection to revolution is entirely contingent. Indeed, liberalism's preferred method is reformist rather than revolutionary, for the latter is likely to overshoot the mark of reason, which is the problem of "revolutionary excess." Conversely, there is no necessary connection of revolution to liberalism. Fascism claims to be a revolutionary movement of the people, even as it targets liberalism and liberals. When we look to the illiberal revolutions of Russia, Cuba, and China, however, we see that there remains a connection of revolutionary self-formation to a science of politics, that is, of will to reason. That connection is a felt necessity, even as the science of politics takes new forms. Of course, to say that the connection of revolution to liberalism is logically contingent is not to deny that there can be very good historical reasons for it.

Fundamentally, liberalism theorizes politics from the perspective of theory itself. This gives us politics as reasoned discourse. The liberal theorist always writes about politics from a first person perspective: he asks what it would take for him to recognize a claim of political authority. He asks this question, however, conceiving of himself as a theorist, not a citizen. He does not imagine an act of conscription but the beginning of a discussion. He wants to be convinced by the logic of an argument; he does not want to be moved by political rhetoric. Thus, he places himself behind the veil of ignorance and asks what it would take to convince him there.

There is no place for the experience of authenticity behind that veil. With that, revolution disappears. The imagined act of discourse, accordingly, assumes that the state has already come into existence. Actual political identity—the historically given—is irrelevant. Liberal theory imagines politics speaking in the voice of everyman and speaking always in the present tense. This is the universal set free of the particular. It is voice of reason itself. Rhetoric, that uniquely political form of speech, disappears. Indeed, the veil of ignorance is a device to disempower rhetoric.

The beginning again of revolution and the beginning again behind the veil can seem to be parallel endeavors. The presence of the former and present of the latter can coincide. To collapse them into each other, however, is a mistake, for one points to will and the other to reason. The mistake is made from both directions: the scholar thinks of legitimacy as a matter of justice; the revolutionary thinks of legitimacy as a matter of authenticity. We would do better to think of legitimacy as a matter of both justice and authenticity, reason and will.

LIBERAL THEORY AND THE ABSENCE OF THE POLITICAL

The counterrevolutionary Donoso Cortes finds the idea of popular sovereignty unimaginable, if not blasphemous. The point of the counterrevolutionary philosophy of the state is not different in kind from that of the Counter-Reformation. Both begin from the proposition that man alone cannot bear the sacred, for man outside of the Church is mired in sin. The political order of a fallen world can never transcend itself; it cannot be the vehicle for redemption, personal or political. This is the position of a theologian who takes up a political stance. It is not a position open to a modern political theology, which begins from exactly the opposite proposition. For such a political theology, the state begins and ends with a belief in the sacred character of the popular sovereign.

The real political-theological problem with the liberal theory of politics is not a failure to grasp original sin but rather a failure to grasp the state's revolutionary origin in the sovereign decision for the exception. Liberal theory does not understand the state's own political-theological origins. The problem is in the dimension of the sacred but not in that of the sectarian.

Schmitt sees that the success of liberal constitutionalism has ironically led to a failure to comprehend the political: "There must no longer be political problems, only organizational-technical and economic-sociological tasks. . . . The modern state seems to have actually become what Max Weber envisioned: a huge industrial plant" (65). In response to this trend of enlightened management of the social, liberalism can pose only "everlasting discussion" (65). To treat politics as just another instance of Enlightenment reason threatens to hollow out the political from within, leaving discourse without decision. To the extent that politics is, in fact, moved one way or another, it is because interest groups see an advantage—usually economic—in that direction. The idea that politics is an autonomous field of meaning disappears in this vision of technology and interest groups: "The core of the political idea, the exacting moral decision, is evaded in both" (65). It is never quite clear whether Schmitt is directing his attack at the liberal state, at liberal theory, or at something in-between that might be characterized as the self-understanding of those who operate in the liberal state, that is, the ethos of liberal constitutionalism.

Schmitt's reasoning is something like this: if politics is not a science, then a commitment to resolve political issues through inquiry will do nothing but produce endless, irresolvable discourse. Talk will not take us to action because political problems are not technical issues of production or distribution. If politics begins at the moment of decision, then it begins just at the moment when the rule-based character of reasoning ends. Liberalism fails to comprehend the nature of the political, because it is committed to an ideal of agreement, first on the rules and then on their application. In a world in which everyone agrees, there is no need for a sovereign voice. Liberalism, accordingly, has no place for the concept of the sovereign. Without the sovereign, however, there can be no decision; without the decision, no exception; and without the exception, we never reach the phenomenon of the political.

Writing in the early 1920s, Schmitt has certainly grasped a fundamental characteristic of liberal theorizing as it was to work itself out over the rest of the century. Habermas's early work is representative of this line of thought. For him, the model of political legitimacy is precisely that of an "everlasting conversation" in which there are no constraints imposed upon the discourse beyond the internal conditions of that discourse's own success.[36] Nothing is ever decided "for good," since there are no limits on what can be brought up for reconsideration and renewed discussion. The same idea informs Ackerman's *Social Justice and the Liberal State*: any claim, expectation, or interest can become the object of a political discourse that asks whether it is just.[37] More than ever, theorists seem to model politics on the open-ended discourse of the classroom. Any effort to cut off debate—that is, to decide—is viewed as a violent act of "silencing." To be silenced is to be excluded from political participation. It is the modern equivalent of the revolutionary claim that current conditions amount to slavery. Liberal theorists' have at their "metaphysical core" a commitment to "freedom of speech and freedom of the press" (62).

In the blogosphere, this theoretical model of politics has achieved a kind of technological presence unimaginable to Schmitt: endless discourse relieved of the burden of ever making a decision. To be active in politics today, for many, is to blog. The disembodied voice can displace every other form of political life. This discursive ideal of political life, however, hardly had to await the appearance of the blog. One of the most important and most famous of modern American constitutional-law cases explicitly identified the paradigmatic form of American politics with the open debate in the classroom.[38] To be patriotic just is to take up the burden of conversation. It becomes a symbol of modern civilization: to displace force with talk, the moment of decision with the endless conversation.

One could describe this situation by saying that liberal theorists are in flight from the decision. Not wanting to exclude anyone or anything, they can never say "enough." Every position and every person must be extended equal recognition, which means equal voice. They assume that, if the conversation continues, eventually everyone will be convinced by the "truth of the matter." There will be convergence. Political conversation is like scientific inquiry: pursued long enough, all participants will move toward a single position, the one that survives all of the criticisms directed at it. We appeal to this idea when we speak of a "marketplace of ideas." In the competition of ideas, another way of describing the open and endless conversation, the ultimate winners will be those ideas that are true—or, at least, true for now. A true proposition is nothing other than one that is no longer debated.[39]

This idea of discursive convergence has powerful defenders in the American understanding of constitutional law—for example, Robert Burt, who models judicial discourse on just such an idea of unanimity.[40] This is not the unanimity of the vote but rather an asymptotically approached end-point of an ideal judicial process.[41] The rules of judicial process are reconceived as structuring a common conversation in which no one is silenced and all participants attempt to convince each other. Its precise virtue is that there are to be no winners and losers, for both sides are to converge at the end of the conversation. Absent such convergence, a decision appears to the losers to rest only on force, not on truth. In that case, it would appear exclusionary, while the liberal community must be inclusive. Judicial process, on this view, may not quite reach Habermas's "ideal speech situation," but the underlying paradigm of justification is the same.

This discursive model of legitimacy appears not only in the judicial process but also in the increasing tendency to establish special "bipartisan commissions" to address problems that appear too difficult for our ordinary political institutions.[42] These commissions are to create a forum for the application of specialized knowledge, but they are not simply panels of experts. They are "bipartisan," not "nonpartisan." Isolated from the everyday corruption of our ordinary political discourse, they are to achieve again those ideal circumstances of discourse that will allow convergence through debate. This is not quite the revolutionary commission of public safety, but it is what happens to that committee once it is released from the circumstances of emergency. That political positions might not converge, that disagreement might be fundamental and irresolvable, is not an imaginable position. The liberal thought is that through the good faith application of reason, every problem has an answer; the revolutionary thought is that the people, meaning those who speak in the voice of the people, can only will the good.[43] In both cases, discourse stripped of the influence of historical contingency and personal interest must always realize the good and the true.

This privileging of discourse goes a long way toward explaining the deep affinities between liberal political theory and constitutional theory. In modern constitutional theory, the free speech clause of the First Amendment has become the ground-norm of the entire constitutional edifice. So much so that there are arguments that it is beyond the possibility of amendment.[44] Liberal theories of constitutionalism, just as Schmitt described, do indeed have a problem with the moment of decision that terminates the conversation. This is the moment that Robert Cover described as "jurispathic."[45] To legitimate the moment of decision, Ackerman, for example, must appeal to revolutionary action itself, that is, to direct action by "We the People." This is a distinctly illiberal moment in his theory, for the sovereign claim to decide is not restricted by any of the substantive norms of liberal theory. While discussion may be a prelude to the decision, we know sovereign presence by virtue of the decision it reaches. As a constitutional theorist, Ackerman cannot be as liberal as he is as a political theorist.[46]

Dworkin as constitutional theorist maintains his liberalism, but to do so he must submerge the moment of decision at the endpoint of an idealized conversation, the internal discourse of that perfect judge, Hercules.[47] A conversation that would otherwise continue without end is brought to an end only by imagining an omniscient figure. Dworkin's ideal of constitutional discourse must be stripped of actual people talking if it is to reach a decision. He, like Burt, would deny the jurispathic character of decision, grounding it instead in the jurisgenerative movement of interpretation. Only in Hercules, however, can interpretation move toward unity rather than plurality.

Liberal theory always comes up short at the actual moment of decision: the judge enters judgment and the losing party is not convinced that justice has been done; the legislature votes well before the debate is actually over, and no one is convinced that the conversation simply worked itself out; the president decides to use force and we are left wondering whether yet another international conference could have avoided the need for the violent act. These moments of decision are so problematic for liberalism because they represent the point at which reason fails but the act remains. At that point, we want to know whether the decision is nevertheless legitimate, since we already know it is unjust.

Politics need not be hostile to reason, but it is a dream of theory to believe that a political practice is the working out of reason. That action occurs before argument is done is not a failing of politics; it is not a compromise with circumstance. Reason simply does not comprehend the whole of the political; it does not offer the sole measure of the decision. That which liberal theory fails to grasp is exactly that which we need a political theology to understand: the sources and character of meaning beyond reason.

CONCLUSION: JUSTICE AND AUTHENTICITY

Liberal theory understands justice as the highest political virtue. But if liberalism offers a truncated vision of the domain of the political, then there are political norms beyond its comprehension. Beyond or apart from justice is authenticity. We know what Schmitt was getting at when we consider the modern bureaucratic welfare state: just as it may be, it strikes many citizens as an inauthentic form of political life. We might think of that as a failure of recognition even in a legal order in which everyone is extended formal rights. By the failure of recognition, we mean there is no place for a genuine expression of the will: there is no novelty, no creation, no personhood. The felt need to break out of this Weberian iron cage poses the real question of the nature of a postmodern politics: Can political life be a domain of authenticity? And if so, at what cost to justice?

Political authenticity, as it emerges in a study of political theology, is that experience of the unity of being and meaning that marks the presence of the sacred. It is the leap of faith in the possibility that we can give up the finite and take on the infinite. Our tradition of the theological—in both its religious and political forms—has always modeled that double moment of destruction and creation as sacrifice. Sacrifice has been our tradition in the democratic revolutions of the past, on the battlefields of the great wars of the nineteenth and twentieth century, and perhaps now in the sites of confrontation with the terrorist.

This inquiry into political theology has traced the deeper thread of freedom that may begin in the exceptional act of sacrifice but extends from there to judgment and finally to discourse. Authenticity is as much at stake in genuine conversation as in revolution. The free thought and the free act are inextricably linked. They stand in just the same relationship to the universal; they both make a claim to the new. Lodged between the free act of political creation, revolution, and the free act of discourse, philosophy, is the judgment. Perhaps we are not as far as we might have thought from philosopher kings. We might think here of Justice Oliver Wendell Holmes who experienced the sacrifice of war, glimpsed the infinite in law, and contributed to the birth of philosophical pragmatism.

Political theology does not ask us to be other than we are. It offers no theory of justice against which to reform our political life. It asks us only to think carefully about our own belief that we are and must be free.

CONCLUSION

Political Theology and the End of Discourse

SCHMITT'S BOOK ENDS WITHOUT A CONCLUSION. I believe he simply does not know what to say: his instincts tell him that liberalism is an inauthentic theory of the political, but an explicit appeal to the counter-revolutionary philosophy of Donoso Cortes would look less than serious. Schmitt appears as a thinker overwhelmed by circumstances. Kelsen, he admits, is more in tune with the times than he is. The future direction of sociology belongs to Weber, not to him. The deep issue his work raises for us, however, is not about the direction of political formation but about the very possibility of freedom—free action and free thought. The defense of political theology has become the defense of philosophy and, with that, the defense of the deepest beliefs and practices of Western culture.

When Schmitt does act a decade later, he chooses authenticity over justice. Anyone who thought that the virtues of justice and authenticity necessarily run in the same direction has failed to understand not just this book but much of the history of Western thought: because man is free, he can be evil. Contrary to Kant, the virtue of freedom is not the same as that of justice.

All of this, I believe, is true. But there is a deeper problem signaled by the absence of a conclusion. Political theology rests on an experience beyond discourse. It rests on faith, not argument, and on sacrifice, not contract. It rests on Kant's third question: in what can we hope? Theory has no capacity to speak the sacred. Theorizing the political may itself be a form of inauthentic political life. The danger is that it will reduce politics to justice. It is like trying to theorize love: any explanation can easily fall into inauthenticity. An authentic *political* theory must be one that simply stops. There can be no conclusion; there is only a pointing beyond to that which theory cannot express.

The effort to collapse the decision into discourse hangs over the very foundations of liberal political theory. Liberalism models the origins of the state in just such a conversation. We can think of the state of nature as a chaotic, cacophony of voices. Only when individuals come together in a common conversation can the state begin. What do they talk about? They talk about the conditions of a just political order. The social contract constitutes the terms upon which their discourse converges. The liberal theoretician is always trying to describe those terms by reimagining that initial discourse. These are the terms that every rational person would agree to prior to knowing any facts about his position in the emerging community. If that conversation could not lead to convergence, then the political community could not begin on grounds of equality but only inequality. Violence would displace discourse at the foundation. The alternative to the social contract is Hegel's master/slave relationship.

These models, however, are not complete accounts of political experience. The experience of revolutionary foundations is captured neither by a model of discourse nor by one of violent coercion. Standing apart from both is an idea of sacrifice. This is the image of Abraham sacrificing Isaac before the incomprehensible command of a sovereign god. Politics, on this view, begins with an act of willing self-destruction that rests on faith, not reason. There is no reasoning with God when He demands sacrifice, for there can be no ambition to reach a common understanding. This is a God whose truth is expressed in his self-description: "I am that I am." The same expression of existence over essence is proclaimed in the readiness to sacrifice: "Here am I."

Abraham's willingness to sacrifice is not a matter of yielding to superior threat, as in Hegel's myth of subordination. God may be sovereign, but Abraham is not a slave. The originating act rests on the faith that through death is life, the central idea of every act of sacrifice. There can be no nation of Israel as a community sustaining itself through history until families are willing to sacrifice their children for the sake of the existence of the state. They do so not because of a promise of their own well-being, as in Hobbes's idea of the social contract, but because they have faith that the state holds forth an ultimate meaning. Sacrifice is the appearance of the sacred as a historical phenomenon. Its domain is silent faith, not reasoned discourse. We can talk forever and never reach a position of faith. This is the faith that connects the transcendent experience of revolution to the jurispathic moment of judicial decision, and both to the state of exception in defense of the nation.

The postrevolutionary state must appeal to both justice and authenticity in understanding its own origins. It has thrown off the master through an act of slave rebellion. Slavery was the prerevolutionary condition of the people. The act of rebellion against the master, however, was simultaneously the appearance of a sacrificial politics of sovereign presence. There is no revolution until there is the pledging of life. Until that moment, revolutionary discourse is just lively argument: the stuff of the classroom or the coffeehouse, not the street. Sovereignty is constituted in the imagining of the sacrificial act: the willingness to kill and be killed establishes the temporal and geographic boundaries of the state. The pledge speaks the same language beyond reason that Abraham spoke to God: "Here am I." The revolutionary construction/discovery of the sovereign is all act, for here speech becomes action.

The postrevolutionary state believes not only that the sovereign acted but that it acted to put in place an order of reason. The sovereign people may speak with the voice of God, but this is an enlightened God who reads his script from political theory. It brings forth not the content of a divine covenant but the content of an Enlightenment understanding of justice. An idea of justice alone, however, has no power to create a political order. No one sacrifices for a universal ideal, which has no locus in space and time. Sacrifice occurs for the particular community—the sovereign presence—even as that community strives to put in place a universal idea of justice. The history of the nation is quite literally the continual contest between these two social imaginaries. Justice alone can offer rules without meaning. Authenticity without justice can produce fascism. In politics, as in our personal lives, we need both love and justice, but that need hardly makes them one and the same.

Politics is a structure of the imagination, which means that it, like every other creative form, combines the particular and the universal. Liberal political theories focus all of their attention on the idea of justice and none on the revolutionary tradition of authenticity. They focus on law, not the sovereign act. But the state is misunderstood if seen as only a forum for debate over the conditions and character of justice. In the modern era, the paradigmatic political moment has been that at which the sovereign conscripts the citizen. Exactly here, one confronts again the sovereign claim on life. One is free to make whatever arguments one wants before that point. One can claim that the use of force is wrong in these circumstances or that someone else should be asked to go. One can argue that it is unjust or that it is inefficient. Abraham could make all these arguments until the moment God decided against Isaac.[1] At that point, discourse becomes only acknowledgment—"Here, am I"—and action is grounded on nothing more than the leap of faith. The modern nation-state extended this demand to every citizen: anyone can be called upon to defend the state with his life.

We are radically mistaken if we think this moment of conscription is behind us. The contemporary war on terror represents the point at which conscription becomes truly universal, escaping even the formal structures of juridification. Conscription can now occur to anyone at any moment: It is just a matter of finding oneself on the wrong airplane at the wrong time. At that moment, there is no further discussion, there is only the act. We exist, then, inside the Schmittian exception. The question is what will we do, not what arguments will we make. To say that this is unjust is not to explain its political meaning. It is not even to begin to approach the way in which the political imagination constructs the violent act as a moment of sacrifice.

Liberal theory believes that for people of good faith all of our political differences can be overcome if we will only remain committed to speaking. But political action always occurs before the discourse is over for the simple reason that the discourse is never over. We become speechless before the command and every command of the state can become one

that demands a life. We cannot know in advance which political controversies might break out into violence. There is no logic to war because
there is no argument that brings us to the point of sacrifice. As long as we
can imagine such a moment of sacrifice, we remain within the political
imaginary. We will not recover a theory adequate to the decision for and
against life unless we turn from political theory to political theology. We
must go back to the beginning and, for us, that is Abraham and Isaac.

Every political sacrifice has the character of the decision. Every such
act is a new beginning in just the sense that the miraculous is always new.
The reappearance of the sacred is a refoundation of the world. The decision is not a moment of thoughtlessness, of a violent flight from thought,
as liberalism would portray it. There is, indeed, something deeply irrational about sacrifice, for it marks the appearance of the sacred in history.
That does not make it thoughtless but only a different form of thought.
Love may be irrational, but that is its virtue as much as its vice. Meaning
comes in more forms than reasoned discourse. The meaning that sustains
an ultimate faith, a faith that can sustain an act of sacrifice, is never a
matter of discursive proof. The only proof that counts is the act itself.

Politics is not striving to be a perfect system of reason. Not reason
but decision describes that most characteristic of all political acts: killing
and being killed for the state. There is no discourse on the field of battle;
there is only the affirmation of faith and the brutality of the act. Just
at the point that discourse ends and the act remains, we need to move
from political theory to political theology. This is the point of Schmittian exception: beyond law is the act. That act neither can nor need offer
a justification of itself. To think that it could do so would be to subject
the idea of the exception to a norm. It would deny the exception in the
same act of affirmation.

There is no way to comprehend that experience of sacrifice from
the outside. Precisely here, we confront the theological imagination as
it enters the domain of the political. A politics of the exception is one
that relies on revelation and faith rather than argument and reason. It
is, as Schmitt writes, a politics of the miraculous, but—and this is the
most important point—it is also an experience of freedom. This is the
moment that liberal theory rejects as a failure of reason. Despite the

failure of theoretical comprehension, the history of the nation has been the narrative of these moments of decision, just as the history of the Jews is a narrative of God's revelation.

If I have been successful, it should now be clear that there is no escape from the act within the law, for even here we cannot escape the moment of decision. Freedom is our burden in action and in speech. The deepest complaint against liberal theory is not that it pushes God out of politics but that it fails to recognize the character of freedom upon which modern politics has rested. At stake in our political life has been not our capacity to be reasonable, but our capacity to realize in and through our own lives an ultimate meaning. Where we find that meaning, we will find freedom. A political theory that fails to see that politics treads deeply on the theological will confuse the political with the bureaucratic and authenticity with justice. It will always be shocked and unprepared for the violence of politics. It is unprepared because it is no longer open to the dynamic of sacrifice, collapsing every turn to force into the destructive act of violence. But sacrifice is always a creative act of destruction; it is the dissolution of the finite in the presence of the infinite. That moment is simply beyond the scope of liberal political theory. It has, however, been well within the experience of liberal states. Simply as a matter of political phenomenology, a theory of politics as reasonable discourse fails to match the character of our political experience as authentically free.

NOTES

INTRODUCTION: WHY POLITICAL THEOLOGY AGAIN

1. Carl Schmitt, *Political Theology: Four Chapters on the Concept of Sovereignty,* trans. George Schwab (Chicago: University of Chicago Press, 2005), 5, 35.

2. See Mark Lilla, *The Stillborn God: Religion, Politics and the Modern West* (New York: Vintage, 2007).

3. *Schechter Poultry v. United States,* 295 U.S. 495, 528 (1935).

4. See, for example, Robert Bellah, "Civil Religion in America," *Journal of the American Academy of Arts & Sciences* 96, no. 1 (1967): 1; Sanford Levinson, *Constitutional Faith* (Princeton, NJ: Princeton University Press, 1988); Harry Stout, *Upon the Altar of the Nation: A Moral History of the Civil War* (New York: Penguin, 2006).

5. For a compelling discussion of some of the less obvious elements of the American civil religion, see Carolyn Marvin and David Ingle, *Blood Sacrifice and the Nation: Totem Rituals and the American Flag* (Cambridge: Cambridge University Press, 1999).

6. "In contemporary discourse it has become commonplace for observers to note that state sovereignty is being eroded by globalization." Stephen Krasner, *Sovereignty: Organized Hypocrisy* (Princeton, NJ: Princeton University Press, 1999), 12–13. See also *The End of Sovereignty? A Transatlantic Perspective,* ed. David J. Eaton (London: Lit Verlag, 2004).

7. Article 15 of the European Convention on Human Rights illustrates the transnational law perspective. It allows parties to derogate most treaty obligations

in "time of war or other public emergency threatening the life of the nation," but nevertheless asserts judicially enforceable standards by which to measure acts of derogation. Measures taken must not conflict with the nation's "obligations under international law" (Section 15), and parties are forbidden to derogate from Section 3 (torture), Section 4 para. 1 (slavery), or Section 7 (ex post facto law). Parties may derogate from Section 2 (taking a life) only through "lawful acts of war." European Convention for the Protection of Human Rights and Fundamental Freedoms art. 15, Nov. 4, 1950, 213 U.N.T.S. 221.

8. Of course, there is no inherent impossibility in the idea of a politically left-leaning study of the sacred and power. The *Collège de Sociologie*, for example, was founded in 1937, inspired by the work of Emile Durkheim, and led by Georges Bataille and Roger Caillois. See Simonetta Falasca-Zamponi, "A Left Sacred or a Sacred Left? The *Collège de Sociologie*, Fascism, and Political Culture in Interwar France," *South Central Review* 23, no. 1 (2006): 40.

9. A recent example was the dispute over the reference to Christianity in the proposed constitution of the European Union. See Philip Schlesinger and François Foret, "Political Roof and Sacred Canopy? Religion and the EU Constitution," *European Journal of Social Theory* 9, no. 1 (2006): 59.

10. For an anthology of some of these writers in translation, see Arthur Jacobson and Bernhard Schlink, *Weimar: A Jurisprudence of Crisis* (Berkeley: University of California Press, 2000).

11. The recent revival of interest has been supported by a number of such studies, including Gopal Balakrishnan, *The Enemy: An Intellectual Portrait of Carl Schmitt* (New York: Verso, 2002); Peter Caldwell, *Popular Sovereignty and the Crisis of German Constitutional Law: The Theory and Practice of Weimer Constitutionalism* (Durham, NC: Duke University Press, 1997); Ellen Kennedy, *Constitutional Failure: Carl Schmitt in Weimar* (Durham, NC: Duke University Press, 2004).

12. Schmitt joined the NSDAP on May 1, 1933. A sampling of the controversy, includes: Joseph Bendersky, "Carl Schmitt at Nuremberg," *Telos* 72 (1987): 91; "New Evidence, Old Contradictions: Carl Schmitt and the Jewish Question," *Telos* 132 (2005): 64; "Carl Schmitt's Path to Nuremberg: A Sixty-Year Reassessment," *Telos* 139 (2007): 6; and Alain de Benoist, "Schmitt in France," *Telos* 126 (2003): 133.

13. Heinrich Meier explores the complex relationship between the place of history in Schmitt's political theology and the experience of history as a demand for decisive action in his own life. Heinrich Meier, *The Lesson of Carl Schmitt: Four Chapters on the Distinction Between Political Theology and Political Phi-*

losophy, trans. Marcus Brainard (Chicago: University of Chicago Press, 1998), 122–73.

14. That an author may not be the best interpreter of his text is a point I develop analytically in chapter 3, where I consider the relationship of freedom to interpretation. This whole project of engaging Schmitt's text illustrates the point made there.

15. Legal and cultural studies that express this interest include Michel Foucault, *Discipline and Punish: The Birth of the Prison* (New York: Vintage, 1995); R. Cover, "The Supreme Court, 1982 Foreword: *Nomos* and Narrative" 97 *Harvard Law Review* 4 (1983); and Austin Sarat, *When the State Kills: Capital Punishment and the American Condition* (Princeton, NJ: Princeton University Press, 2001).

16. Walter Benjamin, "Theses on the Philosophy of History, VII," in Walter Benjamin, *Illuminations* (New York: Schocken, 1968).

17. See, for example, Jacques Derrida, *The Politics of Friendship*, trans. George Collins (New York: Verso, 2006); Chantal Mouffe, *The Return of the Political* (New York: Verso, 2006), *The Democratic Paradox* (New York: Verso, 2009), *On the Political (Thinking in Action)* (New York: Routledge, 2005); Giorgio Agamben, *Homo Sacer, Sovereign Power and Bare Life*, trans. Daniel Heller-Roazen (Palo Alto, CA: Stanford University Press, 1998).

18. Raymond Geuss makes this criticism of Rawls in his essay "Neither History Nor Practice," in Raymond Geuss, *Outside Ethics* (Princeton, NJ: Princeton University Press, 2005).

19. See Elaine Scarry, "War and The Social Contract: Nuclear Policy, Distribution and the Right to Bear Arms," 139 *University of Pennsylvania Law Review* 1257 (1991).

20. I investigate the relationship of law to sacrifice in *Sacred Violence: Torture, Terror and Sovereignty* (Ann Arbor, MI: University of Michigan Press, 2008).

21. No doubt some will charge that my argument is deeply contrary to Schmitt's theory. Heinrich Meier, for example, puts obedience at the center of his interpretation of Schmitt's political theology. (See Meier, *The Lesson of Carl Schmitt.*) I put freedom at the center of political theology. Other Schmitt scholars will object to my disregard of Schmitt's Catholicism; some will accuse me of putting a Protestant approach in its place. Whatever may be true of Schmitt, a political theology of obedience has no place in the American experience. Similarly, if my arguments sound more Protestant than Catholic, that too reflects the American political imaginary. To turn away from Schmitt's interpretation of the text is not, I insist, to abuse his text. It is, rather, freely to engage the text.

22. The term was popularized in Alexander Bickel, *The Least Dangerous Branch: The Supreme Court at the Bar of Politics* (New Haven, CT: Yale University Press, 1962), 16.

23. For example, neither originalism nor textualism, as interpretive approaches to the Constitution, makes a claim about justice. Robert Cover famously explored the tension between justice and law among antebellum judges who personally believed in abolition. He found that almost uniformly they subordinated justice to the demands of law. Robert Cover, *Justice Accused: Antislavery and the Judicial Process* (New Haven, CT: Yale University Press, 1975).

24. Lincoln's Lyceum speech of 1838 remains one of the quintessential expressions of the relationship of law to civil religion: "Let every American, every lover of liberty, every well wisher to his posterity, swear by the blood of the Revolution, never to violate . . . the laws of the country, and never to tolerate their violation by others. . . . Let reverence for the laws, be breathed by every American mother, to the lisping babe, that prattles on her lap . . . .And, in short, let it become *the political religion of the nation*; and let the old and the young, the rich and the poor, the grave and the gay, of all sexes and tongues, and colors and conditions, *sacrifice increasingly upon its altars.*" *The Political Thought of Abraham Lincoln* (Indianapolis, IN: Bobbs Merrill, 1967), 16–17 [emphasis added].

25. For a summary of contemporary forms of American exceptionalism, see Michael Ignatieff, ed., *American Exceptionalism and Human Rights* (Princeton, NJ: Princeton University Press, 2005).

26. See Harold Koh, "America's Jekyll-and-Hyde Exceptionalism," in Ignatieff, *American Exceptionalism*, 111.

27. The United States has refused to ratify the Convention on the Elimination of All Forms of Discrimination Against Women, G.A. Res. 34/180, 34 U.N. GAOR Supp. (No. 46) at 193, U.N. Doc. A/34/36 (Dec. 18, 1979), and the Convention on the Rights of the Child, Nov. 20, 1989, 1577 U.N.T.S. 3. It is hardly the case that the United States, unlike the parties to these Conventions, believes in gender discrimination or denies that children have rights.

28. I elaborate this argument in Paul Kahn, "American Exceptionalism, Popular Sovereignty and the Rule of Law," in Ignatieff, supra note 25, at 198.

29. For contrasting approaches to the ticking time bomb problem, see David Luban, "Liberalism, Torture, and the Ticking Time Bomb," 91 *Virginia Law Review* 1425 (2005) and Alan Dershowitz, *Why Terrorism Works: Understanding the Threat, Responding to the Challenge* (New Haven, CT: Yale University Press, 2002), 158–63. For an extended discussion of this debate see my *Sacred Violence*, chapter 3.

30. Turkish membership poses the question of whether there are religious and cultural conditions of political friendship. Of course, this question can arise internally as well, as it did in the long history of race relations in the United States.

31. "The distinction of friend and enemy denotes the utmost intensity of a union or separation, of an association or disassociation . . . [the enemy] is, in a specially intense way, existentially something different and alien, so that in extreme cases conflicts with him are possible." Carl Schmitt, *The Concept of the Political*, trans. George Schwab (Chicago: University of Chicago Press, 2007), 26–27.

32. Justice Brewer famously wrote that it would have been "puerile and ridiculous to have read a writ of injunction to Lee's army during the late civil war." *In re Debs*, 158 U.S. 564, 597 (1895).

33. Examples of such work include Robert Dahl, *Who Governs: Democracy and Power in an American City* (New Haven, CT: Yale University Press, 2005); Larry Bartels, *Unequal Democracy: The Political Economy of the New Gilded Age* (Princeton, NJ: Princeton University Press, 2008).

34. See Cass Sunstein, David Schkade, Lisa Ellman, and Andres Sawicki, *Are Judges Political? An Empirical Analysis of the Federal Judiciary* (Washington, D.C.: Brookings Institute Press, 2006).

35. See Alec Stone Sweet and Jud Mathews, "Proportionality Balancing and Global Constitutionalism," 47 *Columbia Journal of Transnational Law* 73 (2008).

36. Alec Stone Sweet, *Governing with Judges: Constitutional Politics in Europe* (Oxford: Oxford University Press, 2000). Canada expresses this single horizon of legislative and adjudicative action in section S.1 of the Charter of Rights. Judicial application of S.1 requires proportionality review to justify breaches of Charter rights. *R. v. Oakes*, [1986] 1 S.C.R. 103.

37. As Justice Breyer put it:

[The public's confidence in the Court] is a public treasure. It has been built slowly over many years, some of which were marked by a Civil War and the tragedy of segregation. It is a vitally necessary ingredient of any successful effort to protect basic liberty and, indeed, the rule of law itself. We run no risk of returning to the days when a President (responding to this Court's efforts to protect the Cherokee Indians) might have said, "John Marshall has made his decision; now let him enforce it!" But we do risk a self-inflicted wound—a wound that may harm not just the Court, but the Nation. (*Bush v. Gore*, 531 U.S. 98, 128–29 [Breyer, J. dissenting] [citations omitted])

38. A good example is *City of Boerne v. Flores*, 521 U.S. 507 (1997), in which the Court insists that Congress's power to enforce the Fourteenth Amendment is bound by the Court's interpretation of the scope of the rights protected.

39. The earliest and still canonical expression of the self-identification of the Court and the voice of the popular sovereign is *Marbury v. Madison*, 5 U.S. (1 Cranch), 137 (1803). I investigate how the Court actually accomplishes this imaginative feat in *The Reign of Law: Marbury v. Madison and the Construction of America* (New Haven, CT: Yale University Press, 1997).

40. See T. Alexander Aleinikoff, "Constitutional Law in the Age of Balancing," 96 *Yale Law Journal* 943 (1987).

41. The different approaches of constitutional courts to judicial review is the subject of my "Comparative Constitutionalism in a New Key," 101 *Michigan Law Review* 2677 (2003).

42. See, for example, Bickel, *Least Dangerous*; Eugene Rostow, "The Democratic Character of Judicial Review," 66 *Harvard Law Review* 193 (1952).

43. "Congress can no more interfere with the President's conduct of the interrogation of enemy combatants than it can dictate strategic or tactical decisions on the battlefield. Just as statutes that order the President to conduct warfare in a certain matter or for specific goals would be unconstitutional, so too are laws that would prevent the President from gaining the intelligence he believes necessary to prevent attacks upon the United States." John Yoo, Office of Legal Counsel, US Department of Justice, *Memorandum for William J. Haynes II*, March 14, 2003, at 19.

44. A popular contemporary work that embodies this skepticism in its narrative of the Bush Administration's claims to exceptional power is Jane Mayer, *The Dark Side: The Inside Story of How the War on Terror Turned into a War on American Ideals* (New York: Doubleday, 2008).

45. For a review of the many historical incidents of Presidential deployment of force, see Abraham Sofaer, *War, Foreign Affairs and Constitutional Power* (Cambridge, MA: Ballinger, 1976).

46. In July, 2008, the National War Powers Commission, cochaired by two former Secretaries of State, recommended repeal of the War Powers Resolution of 1973.

47. On the variety of historical forms of contest over claims to speak on behalf of the people, see Bruce Ackerman, *We the People, Foundations* (Cambridge, MA: Belknap Press, 1993) and *We the People, Transformations* (Cambridge, MA: Belknap Press, 1998).

48. On the relationship of jurisdiction to decisional authority, see my *Cultural Study of Law* (Chicago: University of Chicago Press, 1999), 64–65.

49. See Noah Feldman, "Choices of Law, Choices of War," 25 *Harvard Journal of Law and Public Policy* 457 (2002).

50. For an examination of the historical background of this shift see James Sheehan, *Where Have All the Soldiers Gone? The Transformation of Modern Europe* (New York: Mariner Books, 2008).

51. This distinction was popularized in Joseph Nye, *Soft Power: The Means to Success in World Politics* (New York: Public Affairs, 2004).

52. This task has defined the American constitutional project from the beginning. See Paul Kahn, "Reason and Will in the Origins of the American Constitution," 98 *Yale Law Journal* 449 (1989).

53. Lilla, *Stillborn God*.

54. In questioning the "secular credentials" of the modern state, my inquiry shares an orientation with Talal Asad's *Formations of the Secular: Christianity, Islam, Modernity* (Palo Alto, CA: Stanford University Press, 2003). Asad, however, is interested in the political significance of privatizing religion, not the formation of a civic religion.

55. The development of international law reverses this proposition: arguments over the just content of that law have preceded the establishment of any sort of political identity on a global scale. On the significance of this for the status of international law as law, see Paul Kahn, "Speaking Law to Power: Popular Sovereignty, Human Rights, and the New International Order," 1 *Chicago Journal of International Law* 1 (2002).

56. I explore this confusion of theory and experience in *Putting Liberalism in its Place* (Princeton, NJ: Princeton University Press, 2004).

57. Ibid., 38–43.

58. See Charles Gliozzo, "The Philosophes and Religion: Intellectual Origins of the Dechristianization Movement in the French Revolution" *Church History* 40 (1971): 273: "The work of the philosophes was not only to destroy an old faith, but to supply a new faith, which would be in conformity with the new age, to give a supreme significance to the rise of science, the growth of the state and the improvement of civilization" (282). See also Ferenc Feher, ed., *The French Revolution and the Birth of Modernity* (Berkeley: University of California Press, 1990), especially chapter 9 on "The Fury of Rationalization and the Revolutionary Fiasco."

59. Hannah Arendt is reflecting on this—and judging harshly—when she says that the social question, which is the poor's demand for basic welfare,

undermines revolution. Hannah Arendt, *On Revolution* (1963; repr., New York: Penguin, 2006), 54–55.

60. The law and economics school, for example, emphasizes the instrumentality of law to maximize the general social welfare: "economics provides a useful normative standard for evaluating law and policy. Laws are not just arcane, technical arguments; they are instruments for achieving important social goals.... Economics predicts the effects of policies on efficiency.... Besides efficiency, economics predicts the effects of policies on another important value: the distribution of income and wealth." Robert Cooter and Thomas Ulen, *Law and Economics* (New York: Addison Wesley, 2004), 4. For a detailed critique of legal instrumentalism in contemporary American legal academia, see Brian Tamanaha, *Laws as a Means to an End: Threat to the Rule of Law* (Cambridge: Cambridge University Press, 2006).

61. See Hannah Arendt, *The Human Condition* (Chicago: University of Chicago, 1958), 17–21. For a modern application, see Jonathan Schell, *The Unconquerable World: Power, Nonviolence, and the Will of the People* (New York: Henry Holt, 2003).

62. Arendt, *On Revolution*, 37–40.

63. For example, Americans seemed easily to appropriate the language of "homeland" after 9/11.

64. "Each religious person will connect this moral space to his own higher religious goals and ends, but within that space, we are all able to speak a common language and share moral principles. I have argued that this idea of overlap is ultimately more fruitful than the idea of separation, which suggests to religious people that they must give up some ways in which their comprehensive doctrine links the political with the religious." Martha Nussbaum, *Liberty of Conscience: In Defense of America's Tradition of Religious Equality* (New York: Basic Books, 2008), 68.

65. This is the central argument of my *Putting Liberalism in its Place*.

1. DEFINITION OF SOVEREIGNTY

1. Giorgio Agamben argues that Schmitt was writing specifically in response to Walter Benjamin's theory of pure violence. Giorgio Agamben, *State of Exception*, trans. Kevin Attell (Chicago: University of Chicago Press, 2005), 52–64. Whatever one might think of Agamben's claim—and he admits that "the exoteric dossier is not very large"—there is no reason to think that Benjamin's mys-

ticism has displaced Schmitt's larger concern with the problems of liberalism in theory and practice.

2. David Hume, *An Enquiry Concerning Human Understanding: And Other Writings*, ed. Stephen Buckle (1748; repr., Cambridge: Cambridge University Press, 2007), 101.

3. Agamben too notes the analogy of law to language and the relationship of both systems of "floating signifiers" to the decision. Agamben, *State of Exception*, 36–37.

4. Representative works on the nature of legal reasoning include Edward Levi, *An Introduction to Legal Reasoning* (Chicago: University of Chicago Press, 1962); Paul Kahn, *Cultural Study of Law* (Chicago: University of Chicago Press, 1999); Roberto Unger, *What Should Legal Analysis Become?* (New York: Verso, 1996).

5. For this reason, the claim that modern states are moving toward a "permanent state of exception" is always paradoxical. A state will find itself producing, in new ways, norms with the "force of law." See Agamben, *State of Exception*, 32–40.

6. See, for example, Max Radin, "The Doctrine of Separation of Power in Seventeenth Century Controversies," 86 *University of Pennsylvania Law Review* 842, 844 (1938) ("All power was in the king . . . by the king in his courts, in all of which he was present and for every act at which only his writ gave validity."); Duncan Kerly, *An Historical Sketch of the Equitable Jurisdiction of the Court of Chancery* (Cambridge: Cambridge University Press, 1890), 9 ("The King's Courts had originally been established by the King's authority, and their jurisdiction in cases between subject and subject was in every case based upon the King's Writ. . . . The writ had originally no connection whatever with the relief sought, it had been a general direction to do right to the plaintiff").

7. The joining of order and miracle in the idea of God's will was a central aspect of the nominalist revolt against the scholastic tradition in Christian theology. See Michael Gillespie, *The Theological Origins of Modernity* (Chicago: University of Chicago Press, 2008), 36–42.

8. "What is equitable is just, but not what is legally just—rather a correction of it. The reason is that all law is universal, and there are some things about which one cannot speak correctly in universal terms. . . . What is equitable, therefore, is just, and better than one kind of justice. But it is not better than unqualified justice, only better than the error that results from its lacking qualification." Aristotle, *Nicomachean Ethics*, trans. Roger Crisp (Cambridge: Cambridge University Press, 2000), 1137b.

9. See Debora Shuger, *Political Theologies in Shakespeare's England: The Sacred and the State in "Measure for Measure"* (Hampshire: Macmillan, 2001), 82.

10. See H. Brent McKnight, "How Shall We Then Reason? The Historical Setting of Equity," 45 *Mercer Law Review* 919, 934–39 (1994): "In England until the sixteenth century, most involved in the legal system assumed that there was a higher law above the particular laws enforced in any nation; that no nation's laws could be adequate to prevent injustices in exceptional circumstances. They considered the King the font of law and responsible for achieving justice for all the citizens. They viewed him as bound, as a man with a conscience under God, to look to universal laws for guidance both for enacting general laws and for making exceptions to those laws to prevent particular injustices" (934). For the sacral character of the King, see also Bracton's famous saying, "*et minister Dei in terra: omnis quidem sub eo est, et ipse sub nullo, nisi tantum sub Deo.*" ("The King is the vicegerent and minister of God on earth: all are subject to him; and he is subject to none but to the God alone.") Quoted in J. W. Erlich, *Erlich's Blackstone* (New York: Capricorn, 1969), 66. For the King's authority to decide the "extraordinary," see William Lambarde's discussion of the Star Chamber: "As in the Government of all *Common-weales*, sundry things doe fall out, both in *Peace* and *Warre*, that doe require an extraordinarie helpe, and cannot await the usuall cure of common *Rule*, and setled *Iustice*; the which is not performed, but altogether after one sort, and that not without delay of helpe, and dispense of time: So, albeit here within this Realme of *England*, the most part of *Causes* in complaint are and ought to be referred to the ordinarie processe & solemne handling of *Common Law*, and regular distribution of *Iustice*; yet have there always arisen, and there will continually from time to time, grow some rare matters, meet (for just reason) to be reserved to a higher hand, and to be left to the aide of absolute *Power*, and irregular *Authoritie*." William Lambarde, *Archeion: or, a Discourse Upon the High Courts of Justice in England* (1635; repr., Cambridge, MA: Harvard University Press, 1957), 48.

11. *King James VI and I: Political Writings*, ed. Johann Sommerville (Cambridge: Cambridge University Press, 1994), 214.

12. We occasionally locate the virtues of care in the nation when we act toward those in need outside of our community—for example, in response to disasters. We are familiar with seeing ourselves as a single subject—the nation—when acting abroad. No doubt part of the reason we see ourselves this way is because of the absence of a legal regime specifying when such acts are required.

13. On the first, see Ernst Kantorowicz, *The King's Two Bodies: A Study in Medieval Political Theology* (1957; repr., Princeton: Princeton University Press, 1997), 8: "the body politic of kingship appears as a likeness of the 'holy sprites and angels,' because it represents, like the angels, the Immutable within Time." On the second, see Marc Bloch, *The Royal Touch: Sacred Monarchy and Scrofula in England and France*, trans. J. E. Anderson (London: Routledge, 1973); Michael Walzer, introduction in *Regicide and Revolution: Speeches at the Trial of Louis XVI* (New York: Columbia University Press, 1974), 19: "The most extraordinary, though not the most important, power derived from the indelible hallowing of the King—and ritually acted out by French and English rulers from the early Middle Ages until the revolutionary years—was the power to heal men and women suffering from scrofula, the King's Evil." On the third, see Maitland's discussion of the history of equity in which he describes the petition for relief as "often couched in piteous terms, the king is asked to find a remedy for the love of God and in the way of Charity." F. W. Maitland, *Equity, The Forms of Action at Common Law*, eds. A. H. Chaytor and W. J. Whittaker (Cambridge: Cambridge University Press, 1910), 5.

14. See Shuger, *Political Theologies*, 88.

15. Shakespeare, *Merchant of Venice*, 4.1. Reference is to act and scene.

16. Abraham Lincoln, "Second Inaugural Address, March 4, 1865," in *Lincoln's Inaugurals, Addresses and Letters*, ed. Daniel Kilham Dodge (New York: Longmans, 1910).

17. "And the LORD set a mark upon Cain so that whoever found him would not slay him." Genesis 4:11, *The Five Books of Moses: A Translation with Commentary*, trans. Robert Alter (New York: Norton & Co., 2004), 31.

18. This is the inverse idea of the scapegoat, who is innocent yet bears the burden of law's justice. Christ and Barabbas need each other.

19. Grant Gilmore, *The Ages of American Law* (New Haven, CT: Yale University Press, 1977), 111.

20. For example, on his final day in office, President Clinton pardoned Marc Rich, the fugitive commodities trader whose exwife had given substantial donations to the Clinton library and Hillary Clinton's Senate campaign. "Donors and the Rich Pardon," New York Times, March 3, 2001, Editorial.

21. Already by the time of Blackstone, equity had become subject to its own process of normalization. See McKnight, supra note 10, at 938: "Equity was no longer extraordinary by the time of Blackstone and the framing of the United States Constitution. Between the start of the sixteenth century and the end of

the eighteenth century, equity became, in effect, a part of the ordinary law with its peculiar forum, rules, forms and remedies."

22. Schmitt actually says nothing in this text about the locus of the sovereign power to decide. Indeed, he could not as a matter of theory.

23. Tocqueville too linked jury and popular sovereignty: "The system of the jury, as it is understood in America, appears to me as direct and as extreme a consequence of the dogma of the sovereignty of the people as universal suffrage." Alexis Tocqueville, *Democracy in America*, trans. Harvey Mansfield and Delba Winthrop (Chicago: University of Chicago Press, 2000), 261. For a recent effort to link popular sovereign, revolution, convention, and jury nullification, see Michael Dawson, "Popular Sovereignty, Double Jeopardy, and the Dual Sovereignty Doctrine," 102 *Yale Law Journal* 281, 283 (1992).

24. This is why history has no place for past conditional propositions. "What might have been" is not history but fiction.

25. See Jean Bodin, *On Sovereignty: Four Chapters from the Six Books of the Commonwealth*, ed. Julian H. Franklin (1576: repr. Cambridge: Cambridge University Press, 1992), 18–19: "As for laws which concern the state of the kingdom and its basic form, since these are annexed and united to the crown like the Salic Law, the prince cannot detract from them. And should he do so, his successor can nullify anything that has been done in prejudice of the royal laws on which the sovereign majesty is founded and supported."

26. Agamben offers "a brief history of the state of exception" from 1791 forward, tracking its regular reappearance throughout Western Europe and the United States. Agamben, *State of Exception*, 11–22.

27. I explore the connection of the rule of law to systemic completeness in *The Reign of Law: Marbury v. Madison and the Construction of America* (New Haven, CT: Yale University Press, 1997), 170–74.

28. The closest we can come to such an imagination is the extreme nominalist position in which all that puts off such chaos is the continuous will of God to sustain order.

29. As Hart explains: "All rules involve recognizing or classifying particular cases as instances of general terms, and in the case of everything which we are prepared to call a rule it is possible to distinguish clear central cases, where it certainly applies and others where there are reasons for both asserting and denying that it applies. Nothing can eliminate this duality of a core of certainty and a penumbra of doubt when we are engaged in bringing particular situations under general rules." H. L A. Hart, *The Concept of Law* (1961; repr. Oxford: Oxford University Press, 1997), 123.

30. See Ronald Dworkin, *Law's Empire* (Cambridge, MA: Belknap, 1986), 5–6; see also chapter 2 below.

31. Hobbes, for example, wrote of law of nations: "Concerning the offices of one sovereign to another, which are comprehended in that law which is commonly called the law of nations, I need not say anything in this place because the law of nations and the law of nature is the same thing. And every sovereign hath the same right in procuring the safety of his people, that any particular man can have in procuring the safety of his own body. And the same law that dictateth to men that have no civil government what they ought to do, and what to avoid in regard of one another, dictateth the same to Commonwealths; that is, to the consciences of sovereign princes and sovereign assemblies; there being no court of natural justice, but in the conscience only, where not man, but God reigneth; whose laws such of them as oblige all mankind, in respect of God, as he is the Author of nature, are natural; and in respect of the same God, as he is King of kings, are laws." *Leviathan*, ed. Edwin Curley (1668; repr. Indianapolis: Hackett, 1994), 233. For a contemporary realist theory of international relations, see Hans Morgenthau, *Politics Among Nations* (1978: repr., New York: McGraw-Hill, 2005).

32. When they do so, there is often little reason to believe they will abide by the result. Consider, for example, the Beagle Channel Arbitration. On July 22, 1971, the Presidents of Chile and Argentina signed an arbitration agreement submitting their dispute over territorial and maritime boundaries and over the titles to the islands Picton, Nueva, and Lennox to binding arbitration under auspices of Queen Elizabeth II. On May 2, 1977, the arbitrators ruled that the islands and all adjacent formations belonged to Chile. On January 25, 1978, Argentina repudiated the British arbitration and on December 22 started (and aborted a few hours later) a military operation (*Operación Soberanía*) to invade the islands and continental Chile.

33. See Report of the International Commission on International State Sovereignty (2001). The interventionist will likely argue that only the government, not national sovereignty, is the target. That this theoretical distinction can easily fail in practice is one of the lessons of recent interventions in Iraq and Afghanistan.

34. U.N. Charter, art. 51 speaks only of "the inherent right of individual or collective self-defense if an armed attack occurs."

35. See for example, Michael Reisman, "Sovereignty and Human Rights in Contemporary International Law," 84 *American Journal of International Law* 866, 870 (1990); George Soros, "The People's Sovereignty," *Foreign Policy*, January

2004 ("Sovereignty is an anachronistic concept originating in bygone times when society consisted of rulers and subjects, not citizens."). But compare George Soros, *The Bubble of American Supremacy: Correcting the Misuse of American Power* (New York: Public Affairs, 2003), 101: "Anachronistic or not, sovereignty remains the basis of the current world order. It would be utopian to think otherwise."

36. I take up the topic of the temporal character of the legal order in *The Reign of Law*, 69–74.

37. Thus, the American revolutionary leaders understood that the alternative to success was criminal trial for treason.

38. See chapter 2 below.

39. Compare Raymond Geuss, who says that "rather than talking at great length and to no clear purpose about the Is/Ought distinction in general," his purpose is to invite his readers to see "how much more interesting the political world seems to be, and how much more one can come to learn and understand about it, if one relaxes the straightjacket and simply ignores this purported distinction." Raymond Geuss, *Philosophy and Real Politics* (Princeton, NJ: Princeton University Press, 2008), 17.

40. The phrase is discussed by Jacques Derrida in "Force of Law," in *Acts of Religion*, ed. Gil Anidjar (New York: Routledge, 2002), 228. Not even madness is merely arbitrary with respect to norms. The mad, for example, were long associated with a kind of insight. Michel Foucault, *Madness and Civilization: A History of Insanity in the Age of Reason*, trans. Richard Howard (New York: Vintage, 1965).

41. See below, chapter 4.

42. Scholasticism represented a countermove within the theological tradition—a move deeply influenced by classical metaphysics.

43. This point becomes the basis of endless inquiry into theodicy. See Susan Nieman, *Evil in Modern Thought: An Alternative History of Philosophy* (Princeton, NJ: Princeton University Press, 2002).

44. The sign of that freedom, accordingly, is God's absence of knowledge. He does not know, until he sees the consequences, of Adam's sin; He does not know where Adam and Eve are hiding in the garden after they have sinned.

45. In *Out of Eden: Adam and Eve and the Problem of Evil* (Princeton, NJ: Princeton University Press, 2006), I offer an interpretation of evil based on this idea.

46. Carl Schmitt, *The Concept of the Political*, trans. George Schwab (Chicago: University of Chicago, 2007), 26.

47. Ronald Dworkin expresses this idea of the unity of a symbolic order of law in his theory of "integrity," by which he means that we must be able to con-

ceive of the entire legal order as if it were the product of principled choices by a single subject. Dworkin, *Law's Empire*, 254–58.

48. That is the overall topic of Schmitt's *Legality and Legitimacy*, where he explores the paradoxes of power, political struggle, and the juridical structure. Embodying these paradoxes is the case where a "two-thirds majority amending the constitution could use the moment of its majority to decide with constitutional force that certain interests and persons . . . are not subject to change through any type of majority or even unanimity. For an abstract, formal form of thought, that is legal, quite in order, and forever placed beyond the possibility of legal revision." Carl Schmitt, *Legality and Legitimacy*, trans. Jeffrey Seitzer (Durham: Duke University Press, 2004), 53.

49. See *Youngstown Sheet and Tube v. Sawyer*, 343 U.S. 579 (1952).

50. *Rasul v. Bush*, 542 U.S. 466 (2004); *Hamdan v. Rumsfeld* 548 U.S. 557 (2006); *Boumediene v. Bush*, 533 U.S. 723 (2008).

51. The contemporary trend toward juridification of politics has also been seen in the substantial disappearance of the political question doctrine. See Louis Henkin, "Is There a 'Political Question' Doctrine?" 85 *Yale Law Journal* 597 (1976).

52. Recently, for example, the Law Lords upheld a challenge to the legality under the convention of a national act of derogation allowing indefinite detention of foreign nationals. See *A(FC) and other (FC) (Appellants)v. Secretary of State for the Home Department* (Respondent) [2004] UKHL 56.

53. On the political power of networks, see Anne-Marie Slaughter, *A New World Order* (Princeton, NJ: Princeton University Press, 2004); David Grewal, *Network Power: The Social Dynamics of Globalization* (New Haven, CT: Yale University Press, 2008).

54. See Francis Fukuyama, *The End of History and the Last Man* (New York: Free Press, 1992).

55. *Reference re Secession of Quebec*, [1998] 2 S.C.R. 217.

56. See Jonathan Schell, *The Seventh Decade: The New Shape of Nuclear Danger* (New York: Metropolitan, 2007).

2. THE PROBLEM OF SOVEREIGNTY AS THE PROBLEM OF THE LEGAL FORM AND OF THE DECISION

1. Owen Fiss, for example, writes of a need for mediating principles to move from text to judgment. Owen Fiss, "Groups and the Equal Protection Clause," *Philosophy & Public Affairs* 5 (1976): 107.

2. See Cass Sunstein "Incompletely Theorized Agreements," 108 *Harvard Law Review* 1733 (1995).

3. This was the core of Stanley Fish's response to Owen Fiss's theory of "mediating principles." Stanley Fish, "Fish v. Fiss," 36 *Stanford Law Review* 1325 (1984).

4. See Hans Kelsen, *Introduction to the Problems of Legal Theory*, trans. Bonnie Paulson and Stanley Paulson (Oxford: Oxford University Press, 1992), 82–83.

5. Jerome Frank, *Law and the Modern Mind* (1930; repr. New Brunswick, NJ: Transaction Publishers, 2009).

6. See Jed Shugerman, *The People's Courts: The Rise of Judicial Elections and Judicial Power in America* (Cambridge, MA: Harvard University Press, 2011).

7. "The capacity of judges to give meaning to public values turns not on some personal moral expertise . . . but on the process that limits their exercise of power. One feature of that process is the dialogue judges must conduct; they must listen to all grievances, hear a wide range of interests, speak back and also assume individual responsibility for what they say." Owen Fiss, "The Social and Political Foundations of Adjudication," reprinted in *The Law as it Could Be* (New York: NYU Press, 2003), 54–55.

8. This is not to say that the realists generally contradicted Kelsen's positivism. Brian Leiter has argued that their underlying principles are compatible: "The real dispute between Realism and Positivism, in fact, exists at the *empirical* level, that is, the level of whether or not legal rules *causally determine* judicial decisions. . . . Thus, at the *philosophical* or *conceptual* level, Realism and Positivism are quite compatible, and, in fact, the former actually needs the latter." Brian Leiter, "Legal Realism and Legal Positivism Reconsidered," in his *Naturalizing Jurisprudence: Essays on American Legal Realism and Naturalism in Legal Philosophy* (Oxford: Oxford University Press, 2007), 59–80, quotation on 60.

9. Early on, Oliver Wendell Holmes described this approach as the "bad man" theory of law in "The Path of the Law," 10 *Harvard Law Review* 457, 459 (1897).

10. For a modern version of such an equilibrium theory of norms, see Roberto Unger, *The Self Awakened: Pragmatism Unbound* (Cambridge, MA: Harvard University Press, 2007).

11. See Christopher Langdell, *Selection of Cases on the Law of Contracts* viii (Boston: Little, Brown, and Company, 1871): "Law, considered as a science, consists of certain principles or doctrines. To have such a mastery of these as to be able to apply them with constant facility and certainty to the ever-tangled skein of human affairs is what constitutes a true lawyer; and hence to acquire

that mastery should be the business of every earnest student of law." The legal realist assault on the Langdellian legacy unfolded through many decades, but undoubtedly Jerome Frank's attack was one of the sharpest moments: "American legal education went badly wrong some seventy years ago when it was seduced by a brilliant neurotic. I refer to the well-known founder of the so-called case system." Jerome Frank, "A Plea for Lawyer-Schools," 56 *Yale Law Journal* 1303, 1303 (1947). But see Thomas Grey, "Langdell's Orthodoxy," 45 *University of Pittsburgh Law Review* 1 (1983).

12. Felix Cohen, "Transcendental Nonsense and the Functional Approach," 35 *Columbia Law Review* 809, 844–45 (1935).

13. This is so-called soft positivism, inclusive positivism, or incorporationism. See Jules Coleman, *The Practice of Principle: In Defense of a Pragmatist Approach to Legal Theory* (Oxford: Oxford University Press, 2001), 108: "Whether or not morality is a condition of legality in a particular legal system depends on a social or conventional rule, namely the rule of recognition. If the rule of recognition asserts that morality is a condition of legality, then morality is a condition of legality in that system. If the rule of recognition incorporates no moral principles, however then no such principles figure in the criteria of legality."

14. "Reason's ultimate standard is the law we have in us by nature, and law framed by men is law only to the extent it derives from that law. If it runs counter in any way to the law in us by nature, it is no longer law but breakdown of law." Thomas Aquinas, *Summa Theologiae: A Concise Translation*, ed. Timothy McDermott (Notre Dame, IN: Ave Maria Press, 1991), 289 [*circa* 1270, I-II, Q.95, A.II].

15. Nevertheless, there are still some in the natural law camp. The publication by John Finnis of *Natural Law and Natural Rights* (Oxford: Oxford University Press, 1980) gave natural law jurisprudence a revival of sorts. See also Robert George, *In Defense of Natural Law* (Oxford: Oxford University Press, 1999).

16. The problem of systematic, hierarchical unity in law led to Kelsen's interest in international law. Kelsen emphasized that his approach tends "to blur the border line between international law and national law." Ultimately, if "an insoluble conflict existed between international law and national law, and if therefore a dualistic construction were indispensable, one could not regard international law as 'law' or even as a binding normative order, valid simultaneously with national law." Hans Kelsen, *Pure Theory of Law*, trans. Max Knight (Berkeley: University of California Press, 1967), 328–329.

17. Hart holds that a law does not require a coercive sanction to be understood as a law. Therefore, he distinguishes between being "obliged" and being

"obligated." Hart gives the example of stopping at a stop sign when no police or other person is there. You are not obliged to stop, according to Hart, but you are obligated to do so. Likewise, if a gunman insists you hand over your wallet, you are obliged to do so but not obligated. H. L. A. Hart, *The Concept of Law* (Oxford: Oxford University Press, 1986), 79–88.

18. Kelsen's argument is developed in *Das Problem der Souveränität und die Theorie des Völkerrechts: Beitrag zu einer reinen Rechtslehre* [*The Problem of Sovereignty and the Theory of International Law: Contribution to a Pure Theory of Law*] (1920), to which Schmitt refers, saying that it "portrays the state as a system and unity of legal norms, however, without the slightest effort to explain the substantive and logical principle of this 'unity' and of this 'system.'" Carl Schmitt, *Constitutional Theory*, trans. Jeffrey Seitzer (Durham, NC: Duke University Press, 2008), 63. A historically oriented study of this issue can be found in David Dyzenhaus, *Legality and Legitimacy: Carl Schmitt, Hans Kelsen and Hermann Heller in Weimar* (Oxford: Oxford University Press, 1999). See also Hidemi Suganami, "Understanding Sovereignty Through Kelsen/Schmitt," *Review of International Studies* 33 (2007): 511.

19. This critique has been made from both the political right and the left. In "Courting Disaster: Looking for Change in All the Wrong Places," Gerald Rosenberg argues that "[Gay rights advocates] confused a judicial pronouncement of rights with the attainment of those rights." 54 *Drake Law Review* 795, 813 (2006). The battle for same-sex marriage would have been better served if they had never brought litigation, or had lost their cases." Reva Siegel and Robert Post point to the way in which the right engages similarly in a practice of political mobilization through judicial activity in "Originalism As a Political Practice: The Right's Living Constitution," 75 *Fordham Law Review* 546 (2006).

20. We see the same tendency in contemporary international law: agreement on law is thought literally to have displaced sovereignty from the system of reason. See chapter 1 above. For a wide range of arguments supporting this thesis, see Michael Reisman, ed., *Jurisdiction in International Law* (Aldershot, Hants, England: Ashgate, 1999).

21. For a similar understanding of the imaginative function in the creation of multiple symbolic orders of experience, see Ernst Cassirer, *An Essay on Man: An Introduction to a Philosophy of Human Culture* (New Haven, CT: Yale University Press, 1962).

22. "[I]f exceptional measures are the result of periods of political crisis and, as such, must be understood on political and not juridico-constitutional grounds, then they find themselves in the paradoxical position of being juridical

measures that cannot be understood in legal terms, and the state of exception appears as the legal form of what cannot have legal form." Giorgio Agamben, *State of Exception*, trans. Kevin Attell (Chicago: University of Chicago Press, 2005), 1. Oren Gross and Fionnuala Ní Aoláin offer a fourfold typology of the possible relationship of emergencies to law in *Law in Times of Crisis: Emergency Powers in Theory and Practice* (Cambridge: Cambridge University Press, 2006).

23. Reprinted in *Judgments of the Israel Supreme Court: Fighting Terrorism within the Law*, http://www.jewishvirtuallibrary.org/jsource/Politics/sctterror .html.

24. It actually arises before this point, whenever one norm is said to be implied by another, what Schmitt describes as "the formation of a general legal norm into a positive law." Carl Schmitt, *Political Theology*, trans. George Schwab (Chicago: University of Chicago, 2006), 28.

25. The fullest and most comprehensive account of Ronald Dworkin's theory of law as interpretation is in *Law's Empire* (Cambridge, MA: Belknap, 1986), where he characterizes his theory of law as integrity as "more relentlessly interpretive than either conventionalism [legal positivism] or pragmatism [legal realism]" (226).

26. Robert Cover, "The Supreme Court, 1982 Foreword: Nomos and Narrative," 97 Harvard Law Review 4, 40–44 (1983).

27. *Brown v. Allen*, 344 U.S. 443, 540 (1953) (Jackson, J., concurring).

28. This confusion represents yet another version of the desire for unanimity as the ground of a liberal political order.

29. George Priest and Benjamin Klein demonstrated that when parties have similar understandings of the applicability of the law to a given dispute, they tend to settle out of court. When the probability of a plaintiff's victory tends toward 50 percent, the parties are more likely to end up in litigation. George Priest and Benjamin Klein, "The Selection of Disputes for Litigation," 13 *Journal of Legal Studies* 1 (1984).

30. See Ronald Dworkin, "Is There Really No Right Answer in Hard Cases?" in *A Matter of Principle* (Cambridge, MA: Harvard University Press, 1985), 119.

31. Dworkin, *Law's Empire*, 239.

32. I examined the confirmation process as a rite of passage in "Legal Performance and the Imagination of Sovereignty," in *Performance and the Law*, 3.1 e-misferica (June 2006), at http://www.hemi.nyu.edu/journal/3.1/.

33. This idea is elucidated most clearly by the departmentalists. See, for example, Keith Whittington, "Extrajudicial Constitutional Interpretation: Three Objections and Responses," 80 *North Carolina Law Review* 773, 783 (2002)

("Each branch, or department, of government has an equal authority to interpret the Constitution in the context of conducting its duties. . . . [E]ach branch is supreme within its own interpretive sphere."); Michael Paulsen, "The Most Dangerous Branch: Executive Power to Say What the Law Is," 83 *Georgetown Law Journal* 217 (1994).

34. "Jefferson was in accord with Madison on this point, stating that the Constitution should be interpreted 'according to the true sense in which it was adopted by the States, that in which it was advocated by its friends, and not that which its enemies apprehended.'" William Watkins, Jr., *Reclaiming the American Revolution: the Kentucky and Virginia Resolutions and Their Legacy* (New York: Palgrave Macmillan, 2004), 65

35. In the final pages of *Marbury*, the Court works to identify the "opinion of the people" with the "opinion of the Court." I explore this identification in chapter 8 of *The Reign of Law* (New Haven, CT: Yale University Press, 1997).

36. See *Planned Parenthood v. Casey*, 505 U.S. 833, 868 (1992): "Like the character of an individual, the legitimacy of the Court must be earned over time. So, indeed, must be the character of a Nation of people who aspire to live according to the rule of law. Their belief in themselves as such a people is not readily separable from their understanding of the Court invested with the authority to decide their constitutional cases and speak before all others for their constitutional ideals. If the Court's legitimacy should be undermined, then, so would the country be in its very ability to see itself through its constitutional ideals."

37. See Hart, *Concept of Law*, 141–147.

38. Michael Foucault, *Discipline and Punish: The Birth of the Prison*, trans. Alan Sheridan (New York: Vintage, 1977), 222.

39. I offer a similar critique of contemporary legal theory in *The Cultural Study of Law* (Chicago: University of Chicago Press, 1995).

40. Dworkin, *Law's Empire*, 393–97.

3. POLITICAL THEOLOGY

1. Clifford Geertz's studies of the sacred geography of the political space of traditional Bali and Morocco offer good examples of this principle. See Clifford Geertz, "Centers, Kings and Charisma: Reflections on the Symbolics of Power," in *Local Knowledge* (New York: Basic Books, 1983), 121.

2. See, for example, Richard Dawkins, *The Selfish Gene* (Oxford: Oxford University Press, 1976).

3. Francis Fukuyama argued that liberal democracy may constitute the "end point of mankind's ideological evolution" and the "final form of human government." Francis Fukuyama, *The End of History and Last Man* (New York: Free Press, 1992), xi.

4. Here, the contrast between Marx and Engels, on the one hand, and Gramsci, on the other, is particularly helpful. While the founders of Marxism looked for the explanation of cultural forms in the underlying economic structure, the Italian revisionist explored the role of cultural dynamics in determining political and economic structures. Gramsci focused, for example, on educational reform, to which he assigned powerful transformative capabilities: the "advent of the common school means the beginning of new relations between intellectual and industrial work, not only in the school but in the whole of social life. The comprehensive principle will therefore be reflected in all the organisms of culture, transforming them and giving them a new content"; Antonio Gramsci, *Selections from the Prison Notebooks*, trans. Geoffrey Smith and Quntin Hoare (New York: International Publishers Co., 1971), 33.

5. Some argue, for example, that China's movement toward free-market capitalism has been without political democratization. See Minxin Pei, *China's Trapped Transition: The Limits of Developmental Autocracy* (Cambridge, MA: Harvard University Press, 2006); Ellen Bork, *China Syndrome: Capitalism does not Necessarily Lead to Democracy, Weekly Standard*, May 29, 2006; Philip Pan, *Out of Mao's Shadow: The Struggle for the Soul of a New China* (New York: Simon & Schuster, 2008). Others argue the opposite, that development will lead to democratization. See *Reexamining Democracy: Essays in Honor of Seymour Martin Lipset*, eds. Gary Marks & Larry Diamond (London: Sage Publications, 1992).

6. For a popular version of the interplay of these two perspectives, consider Thomas Frank, *What's the Matter with Kansas? How Conservatives Won the Heart of America* (New York: Henry Holt, 2004).

7. See Oren Gross, "The Normless and Exceptionless Exception: Carl Schmitt's Theory of Emergency Powers and the 'Norm-Exception' Dichotomy," 21 *Cardozo Law Review* 1825, 1826 (2000).

8. Gordon Wood sees such a radical and extensive change in the American Revolution: "if we measure the radicalism by the amount of social change that actually took place—by transformations in the relationships that bound people to each other—then the American Revolution was not conservative at all; on the contrary: it was as radical and revolutionary as any in history . . . a momentous upheaval that not only fundamentally altered the character of American

society but decisively affected the course of subsequent history." Gordon Wood, *The Radicalism of the American Revolution* (New York: Vintage, 1991), 5.

9. See above, chapter 2.

10. Approaching the rule of law as constitutive of an entire world of meaning is the theme of my book, *The Cultural Study of Law* (Chicago: Chicago University Press, 1999).

11. Again, like language, we could ask the bioevolutionary question of transition from earlier forms of communication, but this is not a question of the sociology of concepts.

12. See Immanuel Kant, *Critique of Pure Reason* A805/B833 [1781, 1787].

13. Thomas Kuhn, *The Structure of Scientific Revolutions* (Chicago: Chicago University Press, 1970), 5. Kuhn too draws an analogy between scientific and political revolutions.

14. *Planned Parenthood v. Casey*, 505 U.S. 833 (1992); *Roe v. Wade*, 410 U.S. 113 (1973).

15. That difference was marked most of all by the absence of an idea of judicial review in England.

16. For a description of innovations in both directions, see Bruce Ackerman, *We the People: Transformations* (Cambridge, MA: Belknap, 1998).

17. Arendt's focus on natality as central to the human condition is one expression of this theme. Hannah Arendt, *The Human Condition* (Chicago: University of Chicago Press, 1958), 9.

18. Just as speaking to oneself is not a private language, to have a conversation with oneself is to imagine what one might say to another.

19. John Rawls, *A Theory of Justice* (Cambridge, MA: Belknap, 1971), 15–20.

20. For a recent example of a philosophical genealogy of sovereignty, see Jean Elshtain, *Sovereignty: God, State, and Self* (New York: Basic Books, 2009).

21. See Stephen Krasner, *Sovereignty: Organized Hypocrisy* (Princeton, NJ: Princeton University Press, 1999), 12–13; *The End of Sovereignty? A Transatlantic Perspective*, ed. David Eaton (London: Lit Verlag, 2004). See also Edward Rubin, *Beyond Camelot: Rethinking Politics and Law for the Modern State* (Princeton, NJ: Princeton University Press, 2005), 15–18. (Terms of political philosophy such as democracy, popular sovereignty, and legitimacy are actually "metaphors, rather than observable features of the world.")

22. An example of this is Bruce Ackerman's *We the People* saga. It begins with the assertion that "we cannot build a better future by cutting ourselves off from the past, especially when Americans routinely treat the constitutional past as if

it contained valuable clues for decoding the meaning of our political present." Bruce Ackerman, *We the People: Foundations* (Cambridge, MA: Belknap, 1993), 5. His effort to recover the true meaning of American constitutional history through the analytical structure of *dualism* leads him to reject several alternative narratives, such as the competing theories of *monistic democracy* and *rights foundationalism* (7–16), as well as what he calls the *bicentennial myth*, which asserts "the deep continuity of two centuries of constitutional practice" (34).

23. On the importance of rhetoric to legal and political argument generally, see Eugene Garver, *For the Sake of Argument: Practical Reasoning, Character, and the Ethics of Belief* (Chicago: University of Chicago Press, 2004).

24. I explore this connection of freedom to dialogue in *Out of Eden* (Princeton, NJ: Princeton University Press, 2007), 41.

25. In 1969, Schmitt affirmed the centrality of analogy (and architecture) to this work: "Everything I have said on the topic of political theology is statements of a jurist upon the obvious theoretical and practical legal structural resemblance between theological and juridical concepts." Carl Schmitt, *Political Theology II: The Myth of the Closure of Any Political Theology*, trans. Michael Hoelzl and Graham Ward (Cambridge: Polity, 2008), 148n.

26. Arguably, the same processes are at work in understanding natural phenomenon, but we need not explore that here.

27. Job, it should be noted, was a Gentile.

28. That these models of order—for example, creation and law—can themselves fall into a pattern or relationship is the theme of my book *Legitimacy and History: Self-Government in American Constitutional Theory* (New Haven, CT: Yale University Press, 1992).

29. The competing alternative method, proportionality review, tries paradigmatically to close any room for dissent with respect to the basic narrative form: "The nature of [rights understood as] principles implies the principle of proportionality and vice versa." Robert Alexy, *A Theory of Constitutional Rights*, trans. Julian Rivers (Oxford: Oxford University Press, 2002), 66.

30. "If one wishes to realize the distance which may lie between 'facts' and the meaning of facts, let one go to the field of social discussion. Many persons seem to suppose that facts carry their meanings along with themselves on their face. Accumulate enough of them, and their interpretation stares out at you." John Dewey, *The Public and Its Problems: An Essay in Political Inquiry* (1927; repr., Athens, OH: Shallow Press, 1954), 3.

31. Compare *Goldberg v. Kelly*, 397 U.S. 254 (1970); *Arnett v. Kennedy*, 416 U.S. 134 (1974); *Cleveland Bd. of Educ. v. Loudermill*, 470 U.S. 532 (1985).

32. The recent debate over the role of empathy in the judicial decision, which figured in the confirmation hearings of Judge Sotomayor to be a justice on the Supreme Court, moved along the lines of this ancient controversy.

33. Schmitt's actual term translated as "spiritual" is "geistig."

34. Understood in this way, this project runs parallel to that of Ernst Cassirer, who stated that "human culture derives its specific character and its intellectual and moral values, not from the material of which it consists, but from its form, its architectural structure." Ernst Cassirer, *An Essay on Man: An Introduction to a Philosophy of Human Culture* (New Haven, CT: Yale University Press, 1962), 39.

35. This uneasiness with the diverse and the heterogeneous is evident in Schmitt's characterization of democratic equality as a *substantial* equality that existentially precedes and conditions political form and that achieves the form of national homogeneity in contemporary republics. Thus, "democratic equality is essentially *similarity*, in particular similarity among the people. The central concept of democracy is *people* and *not humanity*." Schmitt, *Constitutional Theory*, 263. Equality, of course, always works across difference—how much difference and what kind are issues to be determined in and by actual political practices.

36. Thomas Aquinas outlined a hierarchical Trinitarian theory of divine, natural, and human law, which underlay the integrity of system of law. See *Summa Theologiae* I-II, Q. 72, Article 4; *Treatise on Law* c. q. 90–114. Suarez similarly elaborated a single system of law of which the *author* and *authority* is God; see Francisco Suarez, "De Legibus," in *Selections from Three Works of Francisco Suárez*, S.J., trans. James Brown (Oxford: Clarendon, 1944).

37. See, for example, George Fletcher, *Romantics at War: Glory and Guilt in the Age of Terrorism* (Princeton, NJ: Princeton University Press, 2002), 20.

38. Michael Perry suggests such a conflict: "The morality of human rights is, for many secular thinkers, problematic because it is difficult—perhaps to the point of impossible—to align with one of their reigning intellectual convictions, what Bernard Williams called Nietzsche's thought: '[T]here is not only no God, but no metaphysical order of any kind.'" Michael Perry, "The Morality of Human Rights: A Nonreligious Ground?" 54 *Emory Law Journal Special Edition* 97, 103 (2005).

39. Schmitt, *Political Theology*, 65.

40. That political theory must extend to the relationship of violence to meaning and not speak only to the relationship of law to welfare is the theme of my *Sacred Violence: Torture, Terror, and Sovereignty* (Ann Arbor, MI: University of Michigan, 2008).

41. For an argument that the popular sovereign is the cause of itself along each of these Aristotelian dimensions, see chapter 6 of my *Putting Liberalism in its Place* (Princeton, NJ: Princeton University Press, 2005).

4. ON THE COUNTERREVOLUTIONARY PHILOSOPHY
OF THE STATE

1. The fourth chapter was actually a later addition. The first three chapters were originally part of a festschrift for Max Weber. See Ellen Kennedy, *Constitutional Failure: Carl Schmitt in Weimar* (Durham, NC: Duke University Press, 2004), 78–79n112.

2. John Rawls, "Justice as Fairness: Political not Metaphysical," *Philosophy & Public Affairs* 14 (1985): 223.

3. Leading the critique was Michael Sandel's 1982 book, *Liberalism and the Limits of Justice* (Cambridge: Cambridge University Press, 1982).

4. The continuing association of liberalism with reason is evident in the titles of some recent popular books defending liberal politics against the conservative assault. Robert Reich, *Reason: Why Liberals Will Win the Battle for America* (New York: Vintage, 2004); Al Gore, *The Assault on Reason* (New York: Penguin, 2007).

5. Bruce Ackerman, for example, theorizes social justice as a never-ending dialogue on the justification of institutions and acts grounded on the premise of rationality: "whenever anybody questions the legitimacy of another's power, the power holder must respond not by suppressing the questioner but by giving a reason that explains why he is more entitled to the resource than the questioner is." *Social Justice in the Liberal State* (New Haven, CT: Yale University Press, 1980), 4. Jurgen Habermas too ties the idea of democracy to the rule of law and both of them to the deployment of deliberative reason in the public sphere: "individual private rights cannot even be adequately formulated, let alone politically implemented, if those affected have not first engaged in public discussions to clarify which features are relevant in treating typical cases alike or different, and then mobilized communicative power for the consideration of their newly interpreted needs." Jurgen Habermas, *Between Facts and Norms: Contributions to a Discourse Theory of Law and Democracy*, trans. William Rehg (Cambridge, MA: The MIT Press, 1992), 450.

6. Immanuel Kant, *Foundations of the Metaphysics of Morals*, trans. Lewis Beck (Indianapolis, IN: The Bobbs-Merrill Co., 1959), 39.

7. One cannot trace the line of thought expressed in this paragraph without feeling the grip of the theological on the political. The tension described here

over the nature of freedom could just as easily have referred to the earlier reaction of the nominalists to the scholastics. They too sought to make sense of a free will—that of God—that acted in respect of reason but was not determined by it. They too feared the arbitrary potential of such a will.

8. I investigate the problematic relationship of liberal theory to the faculty of will in *Putting Liberalism in its Place* (Princeton, NJ: Princeton University Press, 2005), 175–78.

9. Tom Wolfe offers a critique of the critics along this dimension in *The Painted Word* (New York: Picador, 1975).

10. Hannah Arendt famously distinguishes the labor of production from action in *The Human Condition* (Chicago: University of Chicago Press, 1958), 4.

11. See the discussion of sociological explanation as caricature in chapter 3 above.

12. This is a critique often directed at the European Union.

13. Ironically, it is the American Constitution's deeply felt connection to an author that creates the possibility of interpretive freedom, including the originalist's position. There is similarly a connection to be made between the rapid spread of proportionality review as a judicial methodology and the increasing skepticism about sovereign authority.

14. Schmitt scholars will see in this distinction a reworking of the contrast Schmitt describes between a normativist and a decisionist form of juristic thought. Carl Schmitt, *On the Three Types of Juristic Thought*, trans. Joseph Bendersky (Santa Barbara, CA: Praeger, 2004).

15. Stephen Holmes, one of today's leading defenders of liberal political theory, writes: "Institutions such as a free press, checks and balances, and periodic accountability before a national electorate can help discipline the stubborn partiality of officeholders. Liberal democracy strives to billet mighty decision makers in conspicuous sites where they can be carefully monitored and where their personal interests will not drift impossibly aloft from the interests of the community at large." Stephen Holmes, *Passions and Constraint: On the Theory of Liberal Democracy* (Chicago: University of Chicago Press, 1995), 5

16. Rawls uses the original position to discern "the principles of justice for the basic structure of society." *A Theory of Justice* (Cambridge, MA: Belknap, 1972), 10. For Ackerman, the decisive moment is that of "constitutional politics" or "higher lawmaking," which is distinguished from the business-as-usual of "normal politics." See *We the People: Foundations* (Cambridge, MA: Belknap, 1993).

17. For a recent summary of the threat of capture and the steps taken to counteract it, see Sidney Shapiro and Rena Steinzor, "Capture, Accountability, and Regulatory Metrics," 86 *Texas Law Review* 1741 (2008). See also Michael Levine & Jennifer Forrence, "Regulatory Capture, Public Interest, and the Public Agenda: Toward a Synthesis," *Journal of Law Economics & Organization* 6 (1990): 167 (discussing the theory that special interests can "capture" regulatory agencies); David Martimort, "The Life Cycle of Regulatory Agencies: Dynamic Capture and Transaction Costs," *Review of Economic Studies* 66, no. 4 (1999): 929.

18. "The problem of establishing a state, no matter how hard it may sound, is *soluble* even for a nation of devils (if only they have understanding)." Immanuel Kant, "Toward Perpetual Peace," in *Practical Philosophy*, ed. Mary J. Gregor. The Cambridge Edition of the Works of Immanuel Kant (Cambridge: Cambridge University Press, 1996), 311.

19. Charles Taylor speaks of liberalism as a "fighting creed" in *Multiculturalism and the Politics of Recognition* (Princeton, NJ: Princeton University Press, 1992), 62.

20. See Charles Taylor, *The Ethics of Authenticity* (Cambridge, MA: Harvard University Press, 1992).

21. For Hannah Arendt the value of authenticity is particularly prominent because it embodies the unfolding of the self through action and words. Of the American Revolution, Arendt wrote: "to find experiences of equal import in the political realm and to read a language of equal authenticity and originality ... in the huge arsenal of historical documents, one might have to go back into a very distant past indeed." Hannah Arendt, *On Revolution* (1963; repr., New York: Penguin, 2006), 173. For Sartre, authenticity, the chief existential virtue, "consists in having a true and lucid consciousness of the situation, in assuming the responsibilities and risks that it involves, in accepting it in pride or humiliation, sometimes in horror and hate." Jean Paul Sartre, *Anti-Semite and Jew*, trans. George Becker (New York: Schocken, 1995), 90. For a fictional representation, see Andre Malraux, *Man's Fate*, trans. Haakon Chevalier (New York: Vintage, 1990).

22. For a popularization of this analogy of the political and the theological, see Catherine Bowen, *Miracle at Philadelphia: The Story of the Constitutional Convention, May–September 1787* (New York: Little, Brown, and Co., 1966).

23. The French *levées en masse* in August 1793, for example, "conscripted" the entire male population. See *The Constitutions and Other Select Documents*

Illustrative of the History of France, 1789–1907, ed. Frank Anderson (Minneapolis: H. W. Wilson, 1904), 183–85:

> From this moment until that in which the enemy shall have been driven from the soil of the Republic, all Frenchmen are in permanent requisition for the service of the armies. The young men shall go to battle; the married men shall forge arms and transport provisions; the women shall make tents and clothing and shall serve in the hospitals; the children shall turn old linen into lint; the aged shall betake themselves to the public places in order to arouse the courage of the warriors and preach the hatred of kings and the unity of the Republic.... They levy shall be general. The unmarried citizens and widowers without children, from eighteen to twenty-five years, shall march first; they shall assemble without delay at the head-towns of their districts, where they shall practice every day at the manual of arms while awaiting the hours of departure.

24. See Martin Luther King, Jr., *Stride Toward Freedom* (New York: Harper & Row, 1958), 216:

> The way of nonviolence means a willingness to suffer and sacrifice. It may mean going to jail. If such is the case the resister must be willing to fill the jailhouses of the South. It may even mean physical death. But if physical death is the price that a man must pay to free his children and his white breathren from a permanent death of the spirit, then nothing could be more redemptive.

25. See Jonathan Schell, *The Unconquerable World: Power, Nonviolence, and the Will of the People* (New York: Henry Holt, 2003), 11: "Only if the faithful were ready to open their minds to the worth and validity of other faiths were they likely to be able to hold to the vow of nonviolence. The test of the 'absoluteness' of faith became not adherence to the exact prescriptions of any sacred text—what today we call fundamentalism—but the willingness to make sacrifices, including the sacrifice of one's life, for one's admittedly fallible beliefs."

26. Jurgan Habermas insists otherwise: "the law of a concrete legal community must, if it is to be legitimate, at least be compatible with moral standards that claim universal validity beyond the legal community." *Between Facts and Norms*, 282.

27. Jefferson said the same thing in the Declaration of Independence: "All experience hath shown that men are more disposed to suffer, while the evils are sufferable, than to right themselves by abolishing the forms to which they are accustomed."

28. For an investigation of the problem of international law to the American legal imaginary, see my "Speaking Law to Power: Popular Sovereignty, Human Rights, and The New International Order," 1 *Chicago Journal of International Law* 1 (2000).

29. Posing the question in this way is not meant to suggest that a chronological account will provide the answer. That would again be a search for causes; it would turn to sociology. Liberal theory was, in fact, already present before the great revolutions of the eighteenth century. Scholars now believe that Locke's political work, *Two Treatises of Government*, was written before the Glorious Revolution of 1688—perhaps in 1683. See Peter Laslett, "Introduction: Two Treatises of Government and the Revolution of 1688," in Locke, *Two Treatises of Government*, ed. Peter Laslett (Cambridge: Cambridge University Press, 1988), 45, 48–49.

30. For an investigation of the importance of these themes to the dynamics of the American Civil War, see Harry Stout, *Upon the Alter of the Nation: A Moral History of the Civil War* (New York: Penguin, 2006).

31. "In order to discover the rules of society best suited to nations, a superior intelligence beholding all the passions of men without experiencing any of them would be needed . . . It would take gods to give men laws." Jean-Jacques Rousseau, *On the Social Contract*, trans. G. D. H. Cole (1913; Mineola, NY: Dover, 2003), 25.

32. Montesquieu, *The Spirit of the Laws*, trans. Anne Cohler, Basia Miller, and Harold Stone (Cambridge: Cambridge University Press, 1989), 22.

33. Compare Aristotle: "Let us assume then that the best life, both for individuals and states, is the life of virtue, having external goods enough for the performance of good actions. . . . There remains to be discussed the question, Whether the happiness of the individual is the same as that of the state or different?" *Politics* 1323b–1324a (trans. Benjamin Jowett).

34. "The very idea of the fabrication of a new government is enough to fill us with disgust and horror. We wished at the period of the Revolution, and do now wish, to derive all we possess as an inheritance from our forefathers." Edmund Burke, *Reflections on the Revolution in France*, ed. L. G. Mitchell (1791; repr. Oxford: Oxford University Press, 2009), 31.

35. See Alexis de Tocqueville, *The Old Regime and the French Revolution*, trans. Stuart Gilbert (New York: Anchor, 1955).

36. "Participants in argumentation cannot avoid the presupposition that, owing to certain characteristics that require formal description, the structure of their communication rules out all external or internal coercion other than the force of the better argument and thereby also neutralizes all motives other than

that of the co-operative search for truth ... [T]hese rules of discourse are not mere *conventions*; rather, they are inescapable presuppositions. The presuppositions themselves are identified by convincing a person who contests the hypothetical reconstructions offered that he is caught up in performative contradictions." Jurgen Habermas, *Moral Consciousness and Communicative Action*, trans. Christen Lenhardt and Shierry Nicholsen (Cambridge, MA: The MIT Press, 1990), 88–89.

37. Ackerman, *Social Justice*, 17.

38. *West Virginia Bd. of Ed. v. Barnette*, 319 U.S. 624 (1943).

39. Unsurprisingly, Habermas has been categorized as a neopragmatist. Indeed, he sets out his reworking of the justificatory functions of communicative ethics by formulating this rhetorical question about pragmatism and hermeneutics: "do they mark the beginning of a new paradigm that, while discarding the mentalistic language game of the [Cartesian] philosophy of consciousness, retains the justificatory modes of that philosophy in the modest, self-critical form in which I have presented them?" Habermas, *Moral Consciousness*, 11.

40. Robert Burt, *The Constitution in Conflict* (Cambridge, MA: Belknap, 1992).

41. This assumption has been a constant target for Jeremy Waldron, who affirms that "in modern constitutional law, the arbitrariness of majority-decision in a legislature is often cited as a way of enhancing the legitimacy of judicial review. In the end, of course, this is a hopeless strategy. Appellate courts are invariably multi-membered bodies whose members often disagree, even after deliberation. When the judges on a panel disagree, they too make their decisions by voting and majority-decision." Jeremy Waldron, *Law and Disagreement* (Oxford: Oxford University Press, 1999), 90–91.

42. Such commissions have been used, for example, to deal with the closing of military facilities, the funding of Social Security, and future problems with Medicare.

43. "It follows from what has gone before that the general will is always right and tends to the public advantage; but it does not follow that the deliberations of the people are always equally correct." Rousseau, *On The Social Contract*, 17.

44. See Jeff Rosen, "Was the Flag Burning Amendment Unconstitutional?" 100 *Yale Law Journal* 1073 (1991); Sanford Levinson, *Constitutional Faith* (Princeton: Princeton University Press, 1988), 150–51.

45. See chapter 2 above.

46. "For the dualist, judicial protection of rights does depend on a prior democratic affirmation on the higher lawmaking track. In this sense, the dual-

ist's Constitution is democratic first, rights-protecting second." Ackerman, *Foundations*, 13.

47. See chapter 2 above.

CONCLUSION: POLITICAL THEOLOGY AND THE END OF DISCOURSE

1. Perhaps a better textual example is Abraham's argument with God to spare Sodom, or more particularly, those who are just in Sodom.

INDEX

War; American Constitution;
American exceptionalism; American
Revolution
U.S. Congress: and exception, 15; relationship with U.S. Supreme Court,
13, 14, 163n38
U.S. Justice Department, and presidential war powers, 14, 164n43
U.S. Supreme Court: appointments
to, 63; authority of, 84, 85–86, 143,
178n36; and civil religion, 9; *Dred
Scott* decision, 58, 86; and exception,
15; and legal form, 62; normalization
of Guantanamo, 54; and popular sovereignty, 13, 85–86, 143, 164n39; and
review of executive decision, 53–54;
source of legitimacy for judgments,
9, 13, 163n37
Universal Declaration of Human Rights,
52
universal human rights, 118, 182n38
universal jurisdiction, 57

violence: Benjamin's theory on,
166–67n1; and defense of sovereign
existence, 11; and exception, 43; and
liberalism, 25, 135–36; political, 7,
16–17, 31, 44; in political culture, 6,
7, 10; and political theology, 17; and
political theory, 182n40; of politics,
158; and revolutions, 139–40; and
rule of law, 19; and sacrifice, 15, 16, 22,

121, 156; and silencing, 148; and sovereign authority, 85; of state creation,
31; of state of nature, 19, 31
Virginia Resolution, 84

Waldron, Jeremy, 188n41
Walesa, Lech, 22
war on terror, 11, 14, 16, 27, 84, 156
War Powers Resolution, 14, 164n46
weapons of mass destruction, 12, 61
Weber, Max, 4, 19, 92, 97, 147, 152, 153
Weimar Constitution, 5, 54, 98, 123, 136
welfare, and law and commerce, 22,
166n60
Whittington, Keith, 177–78n33
will: and citizen, 125; and creation,
128–30, 131; and freedom, 52–53,
62, 75, 77, 81, 97–98, 102, 125, 127;
genuine expression of, 152; and
judicial decision, 63, 80, 97; and
legal form, 75–76, 78; and liberalism,
127, 135; and national existence, 43;
philosophy of, 65; and reason, 39,
40, 41, 48–49, 53, 57, 60, 62, 78, 79,
81, 126, 127, 135, 144, 184n7; and the
sacred, 140; and self-government, 17;
and sovereignty, 32, 35, 36, 40, 47, 50,
51–52, 57, 131, 132
Williams, Bernard, 182n38
Wittgenstein, Ludwig, 68, 103
Wood, Gordon, 179–80n8
World War I, 20, 31